RESEARCH IN MARITIME HISTORY
NO. 7

THE MARKET FOR SEAMEN IN THE AGE OF SAIL

Edited by
Lewis R. Fischer

International Maritime Economic History Association

St. John's, Newfoundland
1994

ISSN -1188-3928
ISBN -0-9695885-6-9

Research in Maritime History is published semi-annually, in June and December. The contents are copyrighted by the International Maritime Economic History Association and all rights are reserved under Canadian and international law. Copying without the written permission of the International Maritime Economic History Association is prohibited.

Research in Maritime History is available free of charge to members of the International Maritime Economic History Association. The price to others is US$15 per copy.

Back issues of *Research in Maritime History* are available:

No. 1 (1991)	David M. Williams and Andrew P. White (comps.), *A Select Bibliography of British and Irish University Theses about Maritime History, 1792-1990*
No. 2 (1992)	Lewis R. Fischer (ed.), *From Wheel House to Counting House: Essays in Maritime Business History in Honour of Professor Peter Neville Davies*
No. 3 (1992)	Lewis R. Fischer and Walter Minchinton (eds.), *People of the Northern Seas*
No. 4 (1993)	Simon Ville (ed.), *Shipbuilding in the United Kingdom in the Nineteenth Century: A Regional Approach*
No. 5 (1993)	Peter N. Davies (ed.), *The Diary of John Holt*
No. 6 (1994)	Simon P. Ville and David M. Williams (eds.), *Management, Finance and Industrial Reslations in Maritime Industries: Essays in International Maritime and Business History*

Research in Maritime History would like to thank Memorial University of Newfoundland for its generous financial assistance in support of this volume.

CONTENTS

Contributors / v

Introduction / vii

CONTRIBUTORS

Carla Rahn Phillips, "Maritime Labour in Early Modern Spain" / 1

Vince Walsh, "Recruitment and Promotion: The Merchant Fleet of Salem, Massachusetts, 1670-1765" / 27

Paul C. van Royen, "Mariners and Markets in the Age of Sail: The Case of the Netherlands" / 47

David J. Starkey, "Pirates and Markets" / 59

David M. Williams, "'Advance Notes' and the Recruitment of Maritime Labour in Britain in the Nineteenth Century" / 81

Yrjö Kaukiainen, "Finnish and International Maritime Labour in the Age of Sail: Was There a Market?" / 101

Lewis R. Fischer, "The Efficiency of Maritime Labour Markets in the Age of Sail: The Post-1850 Norwegian Experience" / 111

Morten Hahn-Pedersen and Poul Holm, "The Danish Maritime Labour Market, 1880-1900" / 141

ABOUT THE EDITOR

LEWIS R. FISCHER is Professor of History at Memorial University of Newfoundland and Series Editor of *Research in Maritime History*. His main areas of research interest are nineteenth- and twentieth-century North Atlantic merchant shipping and maritime labour.

CONTRIBUTORS

MORTEN HAHN-PEDERSEN is Director of the Fisheries and Maritime Museum in Esbjerg, Denmark, and Associate Professor at the Centre for Maritime and Regional History. He has published widely on Danish maritime history in the nineteenth and twentieth centuries.

POUL HOLM is Professor in Nordic Maritime History at the Centre for Maritime and Regional History/University of Aarhus and the Fisheries and Maritime Museum, Esbjerg, Denmark. He has published widely on Scandinavian maritime and regional history.

YRJÖ KAUKIAINEN is professor of Economic History in the University of Helsinki. He has published on various aspects of Finnish and international maritime history, most lately *Sailing into Twilight. Finnish Shipping in an Age of Transport Revolution, 1869-1914* (1991) and *A History of Finnish Shipping* (1993).

CARLA RAHN PHILLIPS is Professor of History at the University of Minnesota. She is the author of *Ciudad Real, 1500-1750: Growth, Crisis, and Readjustment in the Spanish Economy* (Cambridge, MA, 1979), and *Six Galleons for the King of Spain: Imperial Defense in the Early Seventeenth Century* (Baltimore, 1986), plus various articles on Spanish economy and society. She is also co-author, with William D. Phillips, Jr., of *The Worlds of Christopher Columbus* (Cambridge, 1992).

DAVID J. STARKEY is Wilson Family Lecturer in Maritime History at the University of Hull. He has published widely on trade, shipping and shipbuilding in the eighteenth and nineteenth centuries, and is the author of British *Privateering Enterprise in the Eighteenth Century* (Exeter, 1990) and joint-editor of *The New Maritime History of Devon* (2 vols., London, 1992-1994).

PAUL C. VAN ROYEN specializes in the maritime, economic and social history of the Dutch Republic. He is editor of the Dutch journal of maritime history (*Tijdschrift voor Zeegeschiedenis*) and author of *Zeevarenden op de koopvaardijvloot omstreeks 1700* (1987). He is presently Director of the Institute of Maritime History of the Royal Netherlands Navy in The Hague.

VINCE WALSH is presently completing an MA in maritime history at Memorial University. His thesis focuses on the social origins and lives of Salem shipmasters from 1640 to 1720.

DAVID M. WILLIAMS is Senior Lecturer in Economic and Social History at the University of Leicester. A specialist in nineteenth-century British maritime and economic history, he is co-editor of *Management, Finance and Industrial Relations in Maritime Industries: Essays in International Maritime and Business History* (*RIMH*, No. 6, 1994).

Introduction

Lewis R. Fischer

This book had its genesis in an invitation from the Executive of the International Economic History Association. Through its Secretary-General, Professor Joseph Goy, I was invited two years ago to organize a session at the Eleventh International Congress of Economic History in Milan, Italy, in September 1994 to deal with issues raised in Charles Kindleberger's recent book, *Mariners and Markets*. As might be expected from a scholar with a wide-ranging intellect and eclectic interests, Professor Kindleberger raised a myriad of questions in his short but provocative volume. While many of these will hopefully stimulate further research, to provide a focus for the session (and for this book) I asked contributors to focus principally on two related considerations: did markets for seafarers exist in the age of sail; and, if so, were they efficient? As readers will soon discover, I provided no fixed definition of the term "efficiency."

The papers collected here were first presented at the Milan conference. But they are not simply a collection of conference papers, since the participants were all invited to participate on the basis of their expertise on the topic. Indeed, all had written on historical maritime labour markets or were currently in the midst of major projects in which this topic was a key component. In short, this book brings together insights from many of the most prominent students of the subject. Again, to provide some coherence, I limited participants to the North Atlantic, broadly defined. There is obviously a need for a broader exploration of the theme, but this is not the place for it.

I was honoured by the invitation to organize this symposium, since Charles Kindleberger has without question been one of the most important economic historians of the past half-century. Although he has not written extensively on maritime affairs, he has long been a member of the International Maritime Economic History Association. Moreover, he comes by his interest in maritime issues honestly: as readers of

Mariners and Markets will know, like the recent Nobel laureate, Douglass C. North, Charles Kindleberger put in a stint at sea in his youth. If his scholarly priorities took him away from asking maritime questions for most of his career, they clearly did not prevent him from thinking about such things. *Mariners and Markets*, among its other great virtues, will doubtless impel more economic historians to consider transport issues in their work.

The eight essays in this volume are divided temporally into two sections: the first four focus on what we can think of broadly as the early-modern period while the final four examine the nineteenth-century. The early-modern essays collectively come close to answering one question while failing to achieve a consensus on the other. None of the authors seriously doubts the existence of maritime labour markets, although there is less agreement on their spatial extent or efficiency. Carla Rahn Phillips of the University of Minnesota finds that although for most of the early-modern era "a market for maritime labour functioned in Spain," its efficiency was "blunted" by a variety of factors. Vince Walsh of Memorial University of Newfoundland argues that in seventeenth- and eighteenth-century Salem, Massachusetts, "a maritime labour market operated efficiently." Yet "because outsiders were generally excluded," he concludes, the market's efficiency was still by some standards less than optimal. Paul van Royen, Director of the Institute of Maritime History in The Hague, finds at least two markets in the late seventeenth- and early eighteenth-century Netherlands, differentiated at least in part spatially. But van Royen also questions the validity of the concept of efficiency as it has been applied to historical settings, arguing that it may obscure more than it reveals. Similarly, David Starkey of the University of Hull finds a variety of markets in eighteenth-century England. For pirates, the group upon which he focuses, he finds a relatively efficient market at some times but a much less effective one at others. In their divisions over how well markets worked, the authors reflect, at least in part, some of the ambivalence among economists and economic historians in general over the definition of "efficiency."

The same kinds of disagreements are apparent in the essays on the nineteenth century. David Williams of the University of Leicester describes the history and impact of the advance note in Britain, showing how it shaped market behaviour. Given the ease with which notes could

Introduction

affect behaviour, at least in Britain, through much of the century, it seems unlikely that efficient markets existed. Yrjö Kaukiainen of the University of Helsinki contends that in the late nineteenth-century there was "a network of more or less connected local maritime labour markets" in Finland. Whether or not these markets were efficient, he contends, depends upon the definition of term being applied. In an outgrowth of some earlier work I did with Helge Nordvik, I argue that there were local maritime labour markets in pre-World War I and some evidence of integration into regional markets in the southern part of the country. Yet by most criteria, I do not believe that these markets can be called efficient. Finally, Morten Hahn-Pedersen and Poul Holm argue that there were distinct markets for fishing and shipping in late nineteenth-century Denmark. The pattern of wages, however, does not suggest that the markets were terribly efficient.

The rapid appearance of these essays would not have been possible without cooperation from a number of people. All the authors agreed to work to some fairly strict time parameters – and most delivered. I thank them for their willingness to put aside competing obligations to make revisions and to correct proofs. Similarly, we had to ask our referees to provide input in an extremely compressed time frame. Since they do their work anonymously, it is not possible to thank them by name, but suffice it to say that they too performed well under considerable time pressures. As always, Margaret Gulliver managed to organize the papers, format and typeset them, and get them into the hands of our printers with an efficiency that stands in sharp distinction to some of the markets described in the following papers.

Maritime Labour in Early Modern Spain

Carla Rahn Phillips

From the late fifteenth to the early nineteenth century, the duration of Spain's imperial heyday, ocean-going ships provided crucial links between the home country and its colonies around the globe. Trading voyages across the Atlantic and Pacific, as well as within Europe, accounted for an overwhelming majority of the demand for sailors over those three centuries. Military needs added substantially, especially during the frequent wars of the early modern period. Mariners were also needed for Spain's coastal fisheries and for more distant voyages in pursuit of cod and whales. How were these demands matched with the supply of mariners? Or, put another way, to what extent did a labour market for sailors function in Spain during the early modern era?

Any approach to this question involves comparisons among several elements: on one hand, population size and trends, the importance of other occupations (especially agriculture), and the availability of nautical skills in the workforce; on the other, total demand for mariners, given the relative importance of commerce and warfare. Wage levels in agriculture, industry, service, and maritime occupations would let us examine whether remuneration played a dominant role in matching supply with demand. The sources provide surprisingly detailed information about some of these elements, but very little on others. Because government records are far better preserved than private accounts, we know more about crews on royal ships than on private merchantmen. Moreover, historical scholarship has served some regions of early modern Spain better than others, leaving discouraging gaps. For instance, Galicia in northwest Spain, with a long seafaring tradition, has been much better studied than the Basque province of Vizcaya, which had an equally intimate connection with the sea. In the analysis that follows, I will discuss several factors that defined the market for maritime labour in early modern Spain: demographic and economic trends, the number of mariners, the total tonnage of shipping, and the level of maritime wages.

Research in Maritime History, No. 7 (December 1994), 1-25.

Table 1
Spanish Population by Region (In Thousands)

Regions	Maritime Area	1530	1591	c.1740	1768	1787
Aragon	0	255	310	495	530	623
Extremadura	0	305	451	301	273	417
Leon	0	503	633	605	600	628
New Castile	0	614	1,145	1,133	1,131	1,142
Old Castile	0	1,049	1,254	1,022	978	1,232
Asturias	1	81	133	360	403	348
Basque Country and Navarre	1	268	296	404	425	535
Galicia	1	263	504	995	1,088	1,346
Catalonia	2	251	364	796	878	899
Murcia	2	74	115	285	317	338
Valencia	2	273	360	678	739	783
Andalucia	3	762	1,067	1,566	1,661	1,847
Total		4,698	6,632	8,640	9,023	10,138
Areas with Coastline		1,972	2,839	5,084	5,511	6,096
North Coast (Area 1)		612	933	1,759	1,916	2,229
East Coast (Area 2)		598	839	1,759	1,934	2,020
South Coast (Area 3)		762	1,067	1,566	1,661	1,847
Inland Areas		2,726	3,793	3,556	3,512	4,042
Percent Inland		58	57	41	39	40
Percent near the Coasts		42	43	59	61	60

Note: Data for 1740 are interpolated.

Source: Jordi Nadal, "La población española durante los siglos XVI, XVII y XVIII. Un balance a escala regional," in Vicente Pérez Moreda and David-Sven Reher (eds.), *Demografía histórica en España* (Madrid, 1988), 40.

**Figure 1
Spain**

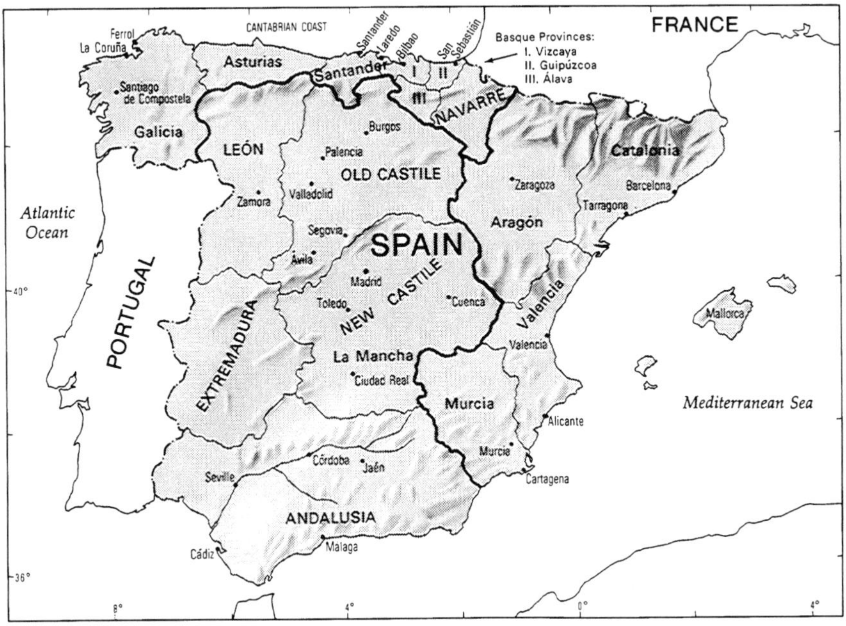

Source: Courtesy of the author.

General Population

The first item that must be considered – in this topic as in most others – is the size and trends of the population. Although Spain's maritime industries habitually employed some foreign ships and men, the vast majority of sailors were native-born. The size of the Spanish population is therefore a key element in examining the labour market (see table 1). Reliable household counts do not appear much before the early sixteenth century. The best censuses for the sixteenth century date from 1528-1530 and 1591, and have the added merit of including regional totals.[1] The on-going debate about an ideal multiplier to convert household figures to inhabitants currently favours four, or even less, although a case can be made for five as well. Based on fairly reliable figures for households and

---

[1]See Annie Molinié-Bertrand, *Au siècle d'or: L'Espagne et ses hommes: La Population du Royaume de Castille au XVIe siècle* (Paris, 1985), 308-309.

using a multiplier of four, Spain had about 4.7 million persons in 1530 and about 6.6 million in 1591. The fastest-growing regions were New Castile in the centre of the country, and Galicia and Asturias in the northwest. Although no region declined in population during the sixteenth century, the Basque country and Navarre in the north grew least. In other words, two classic areas of maritime recruitment – Galicia and the Basque country – showed great disparity in population behavior during the sixteenth century. The other coastal areas – Andalusia in the southwest, and Catalonia and Valencia on the Mediterranean – experienced notable growth in the same period.[2]

Historians agree that the sixteenth century saw extraordinary population growth in Spain, as in the rest of Europe, yet just how long this lasted is a matter of considerable debate. Elsewhere I have argued that the limits of growth were reached in Castile sometime in the 1570s and at about the same time in the north. In the eastern area of the Crown of Aragon, which held about fourteen percent of the total population of Spain, growth seems to have persisted until about 1610-1620, sustained in part by French immigration.[3] A serious epidemic (1599-1601) affected many areas of Spain, worsening the population crisis that had already begun. Recent summaries of work on Spanish population generally confirm this timetable.[4]

Once the limits of growth had been reached, the Spanish population entered a period of stagnation, followed by a decline in the early seventeenth century that varied in duration by region. Unfortunately, we lack reliable census data for the seventeenth century, although baptismal registers enable us to estimate trends. Based on baptismal records for 115 parishes throughout Spain, Jordi Nadal recently argued that inland regions did not return to sixteenth-century birth rates until well into the eighteenth century. By contrast, some coastal regions experienced a resurgence of birth rates by the mid-to-late seventeenth century, earliest in the case of Galicia, followed by Andalusia and then

---

[2]Jordi Nadal, "La población española durante los siglos XVI, XVII y XVIII. Un balance a escala regional," in Vicente Pérez Moreda and David-Sven Reher (eds.), *Demografía histórica en España* (Madrid, 1988), 39-40.

[3]Carla Rahn Phillips, "Time and Duration: A Model for the Economy of Early Modern Spain," *American Historical Review*, XCII (June 1987).

[4]See the brief summary articles in Moreda and Reher (eds.), *Demografía histórica*.

Catalonia. Birth rates alone cannot define the rate of population growth, but it would seem that the coastal areas had begun to show more demographic buoyancy than the interior by the late seventeenth century, even though the latter still contained the vast majority of people. I have argued that the population probably began to turn upward by the mid-seventeenth century in much of Spain, and a variety of indicators suggests that a general recovery was under way by about 1680.[5]

The eighteenth century was marked by another strong population rise, which is well-documented in its later stages. Censuses considered reliable record an increase from nine to about 10.1 million inhabitants between 1768 and 1787. Considering that the overall population probably fell in the early seventeenth century, and recovered slowly, its rise to nine million by 1768 suggests very strong growth in the early eighteenth century, though that growth was by no means uniform. The coastal regions of Asturias, Murcia, and Catalonia showed the strongest increases between 1591 and 1768, but several parts of the Castilian heartland registered declines or, more accurately, had still not recovered from the seventeenth-century slump by 1768, although their levels of baptisms rose from the mid-seventeenth century. By 1787, every region but two had surpassed their 1591 population, and the two laggards had nearly done so.

Between 1591 and 1740, Spanish population underwent a significant redistribution. Inland regions held about sixty percent of the total in 1591, and regions with extensive coastlines held the remaining forty percent. Before 1750 the proportions had reversed, and coastal regions would retain sixty percent of the population for the rest of the eighteenth century. The shift seems to have been related to the global economy, in which the growing importance of trade tended to favour the coasts.

Economic Trends[6]

Population changes underlay trends in the Spanish economy, especially in agriculture. In sixteenth-century Castile, the population rise stimulated an expansion of cultivation, often at the expense of traditional pastures

---

[5]Phillips, "Time and Duration."

[6]The discussion that follows stems from *ibid.* and the sources cited therein. A more recent summary of the evidence is in Moreda and Reher (eds.), *Demografía histórica*.

and rights-of-way for migratory flocks of sheep. Nonetheless, for a time agriculture and herding both expanded, until a Malthusian crisis brought the upward spiral of population and agricultural output to a halt. Over the long term, the low population density and plentiful land in Castile were not conducive to agricultural innovation.

Castilian industry grew impressively in the sixteenth century, particularly textile manufacturing but also metallurgy, paper production, soapmaking, and fish salting. Shipbuilding grew in response to the needs of the empire, as well as the demands of intra-European trade. A bit later, I will discuss the size and tonnage of Spain's Atlantic fleets. Profits from trade with the Indies seem to have flowed into both agriculture and industry in Castile, as well as funding empire-building in the Americas. Castilian industry expanded until rising prices for agricultural products restricted the market for manufactures, probably by about 1600.

During the seventeenth century, Castilian agriculture contracted, some land was returned to pasture, and many farmers turned to market crops, such as grapes, olives, and fruits that promised better returns. Much of the history of Castilian manufacturing remains to be written, but the emerging story contains some fascinating paradoxes. Traditional hubs of textile production, such as Segovia and Toledo, experienced a near-total collapse, but there is evidence that smaller centres and rural areas increased their production of cloth during the seventeenth century, benefiting from the increased availability of wool. Large-scale transhumant herding, under the jurisdiction of the flockowners' association known as the Mesta, seems to have declined during the seventeenth century, but localized herding and short-distance transhumance seem to have increased notably, redefining a centuries-old pattern of rural land use in Castile. Agriculture and, to a lesser extent, manufacturing revived along with population from the late seventeenth century, experiencing notable growth in the eighteenth. By the late eighteenth century, population growth once again approached the limits of the food supply, but this time it would not be cut back. Instead, the economy would expand enough to sustain a steadily growing population, but in conditions very close to the subsistence level.

Landholdings in the humid north historically tended to be smaller than on the plains of Castile, and the dense population often had difficulty growing sufficient grain. Population growth in the sixteenth century, followed by harvest crises and epidemics, encouraged patterns of out-migration, later marriages, and agricultural innovation. Part of the long-term rise in population in Spain's northern regions, especially

Asturias, stemmed from the introduction of maize, potatoes, and other new crops during the seventeenth century, which together could support denser human and animal populations. Still, increasing strains on the local resource base reached crisis proportions by the late eighteenth century. As in Castile, the population continued to grow, but very slowly, consciously restrained by out-migration, late marriages and low levels of fertility. In the late eighteenth century, women in Galicia and the Basque country were older at marriage than women anywhere else in Spain.[7]

In the eastern part of the Iberian peninsula, similar factors combined to keep the population in line with available resources. Over the long term, population grew moderately, sustained by food imports in critical years and restrained by periodic epidemics. A seventeenth-century crisis in industry paralleled that in Castile, although it was more closely tied to the European slump than to events in the Iberian interior. Agricultural and industrial revival from the late seventeenth century marked the beginning of Catalonia's modern career in industry and overseas trade, with growth in the eighteenth century leading to the region's industrial prominence. Overall, the constituent parts of Spain's economy experienced similar trends from the sixteenth through the eighteenth centuries, although each region responded to the changing situation rather differently, depending upon the local resource base. The inland areas experienced dramatic economic and demographic fluctuations throughout. The coastal areas, for the most part, experienced a more moderate cycle of growth and retrenchment and adopted behaviours, such as delayed marriage and the temporary or permanent migration of surplus males, that tended to protect the population from extreme fluctuations. Maritime employment was an important part of out-migration.

The Maritime Population

Overall trends in Spanish demographic and economic history were broadly related to the market for mariners, despite the fact that the vast majority of seamen came from the coastal regions. The relationship between coastal Spaniards and the sea was rooted in both geography and

---

[7]Robert Rowland, "Sistemas matrimoniales en la Península Ibérica (siglos XVI-XIX). Una perspectiva regional," in Moreda and Reher (eds.), *Demografía histórica*, 95.

ancient history. The Atlantic coastlines of the north and southwest, and the Mediterranean shores of the east and southeast, featured hundreds of large and small ports, havens for fishermen, traders, and pirates for millennia. In coastal towns, maritime skills were often passed from generation to generation, and the majority of the population was often connected with the sea to some degree. Since government and entrepreneurs in early modern times counted on this reservoir of experienced seafarers to supply their needs, it was a matter of national concern that seafaring traditions be maintained. In the late sixteenth century, mariners in the Indies trades came disproportionately from Andalusia, the gateway to Spain's American empire (see table 2). By contrast, nearly half the sailors in the Atlantic naval fleets came from Cantabria, and another forty-two percent from Andalusia (see table 3).[8] Presumably, both mercantile and naval voyages in the Mediterranean relied heavily on mariners from the east coast.

Table 2
Origins of Mariners on Spanish
Naval Vessels, 1573-1593

Origin	Total Mariners	Percent	Officers	Percent	Gunners & Mariners	Percent
Cantabria	352	49.9	81	49.1	271	50.2
Andalusia	294	41.7	68	41.2	226	41.9
Castile	34	4.8	13	7.9	21	3.9
Aragon	20	2.8	3	1.8	17	3.1
Canary Is.	5	0.7	0	0.0	5	0.9
Total	705	100.0	165	100.0	540	100.0

Source: Pablo Emilio Pérez-Mallaína Bueno, *Los hombres del Océano. Vida cotidiana de los tripulantes de las flotas de Indias. Siglo XVI* (Seville, 1992), 71.

The need for crews for merchantmen, fishing vessels, and naval ships rose dramatically in the sixteenth century, but as long as the population was rising, the supply of mariners expanded as well. In the early seventeenth century, however, as population fell, the crown became

---

[8]Pablo Emilio Pérez-Mallaína Bueno, *Los hombres del Océano. Vida cotidiana de los tripulantes de las flotas de Indias. Siglo XVI* (Seville, 1992), 61 and 71, notes 71 and 72.

worried about the next generation of sailors. A royal document in late October of 1625 urged all mariners to register with officials in their home ports, so that the government could keep track of them. The king took pains to promise that registration would neither hinder their ability to work on merchant vessels nor bind them to serve in royal fleets unless they volunteered. The principle of voluntary levies would be maintained. The registrants would merely be obligated to give notice of any plans to be absent from home. In return for accepting such inconveniences, each registrant would enjoy an attractive list of privileges and exemptions. Most important, they and their property would be shielded from seizure for debt in most circumstances. They could also bear arms anywhere in the realm and their homes would be exempt from the requirement to billet soldiers and government officials. At sea, they were supposed to be given preferential treatment on both royal and private vessels, benefits that the House of Trade in Seville was charged with enforcing. As an inducement for families to send their sons to sea, a father with four sons serving on royal fleets would gain exemption from all personal taxes. Even if two died, the exemption would continue as long as the other two remained in royal service.[9]

Table 3
Origins of Mariners on Spanish
Merchant Vessels, 1593-1594

Origin	Total Mariners	Percent	Officers	Percent	Gunners & Mariners	Percent
Cantabria	238	11.5	36	9.4	202	12.0
Andalusia	1,619	78.5	309	80.5	1,310	78.0
Castile	80	3.9	12	3.1	68	4.1
Aragon	99	4.8	16	4.2	83	4.9
Canary Is.	27	1.3	11	2.9	16	1.0
Total	2,063	100.0	384	100.0	1,679	100.0

Source: See table 2.

The registration system does not seem to have gone into effect in 1625, however. Although war with the rebellious Netherlands had resumed in 1621, perhaps the general slump in the economy lessened the

---

[9]Archivo General de Simancas (AGS), Secretaría de Marina, legajo (leg.) 276.

demand for mariners enough so that the existing supply was sufficient, although we have no firm figures for the size of that supply. A single sheet folded in with the 1625 decree estimated the number of mariners in all of Spain. Unfortunately, it is not dated, and the decree is currently filed among papers for 1730-1738. The undated estimate included mariners in all the towns along the coast and up to one league (about four miles) inland, in addition to foreigners who might volunteer for Spanish service (see table 4). It also included potential apprentice seamen such as children who had been abandoned, orphaned, or mistreated ("*mal entretenidos*") in the large cities. In all, the list estimated 30,000 mariners of all sorts who might be registered, with over twenty percent from Galicia. Assuming that the estimate dated from 1625, the Galician figure was only about 1.3% of the region's population, albeit a much higher percentage of the 120 or so coastal towns. The percentages for Guipúzcoa, Catalonia, and Murcia are nearly identical. While figures are lacking for Vizcaya, there is no doubt that Bilbao and nearby coastal villages also contained a significant population of mariners.

As the Thirty Years' War continued, Spain found itself fighting a naval war against not only the Dutch but also the French from 1635. Seaborne trade with America also needed merchant vessels and naval escorts. In 1639-1640 there was a special urgency to naval recruitment, as Spain prepared fleets to fight France and the Netherlands. In Spain, recruiters encountered shortages of qualified mariners in 1640; when Spanish agents abroad negotiated to charter alien vessels, they also recruited foreign crews, in particular from Ragusa, Naples, and Genoa.[10]

After the Thirty Years' War, France replaced Spain as the dominant power in Europe, and the latter fought numerous defensive wars against French aggression in the late seventeenth century, although with a minimal maritime dimension. When the last of the Spanish Habsburgs died in 1700, the succession of a French Bourbon to the Spanish throne provoked a lengthy war (1701-1713) with a considerable naval component. Spain could afford only twenty-eight galleys in the Mediterranean and twenty warships in her Atlantic fleet, the latter heavily committed to the protection of the empire. Consequently, she

---

[10]AGS, Guerra Antigua, legs. 3176-3178.

relied heavily on Bourbon France to supply additional seapower.[11] As was traditional, crews for the Spanish ships were for the most part recruited voluntarily, and were levied only in the most urgent circumstances, through quotas assigned to municipal authorities.

The supply of mariners seems to have been sufficient to meet demand during the first two decades of the eighteenth century even with the Indies trade beginning to recover. By the 1720s, however, the situation began to change. The growth of intra-European trade, the needs of the empire, the campaign to recover possessions in Italy lost after the War of Succession, and the increasing rivalry with England evidently persuaded the government to revive plans to register the maritime population. Spanish authorities believed that voluntary recruitment was superior to forced levies carried out in an atmosphere of crisis. A registry of experienced mariners would enable more efficient recruitment when the need arose.[12] A royal order of 29 August 1726 offered exemption from army levies to all mariners who registered with their local authorities.[13] Various documents from 1734 indicate that it remained difficult to supply men for a fleet forming in Cádiz. One report mentioned two ships that had lost about a third of their crews through desertions, deaths, illness or injury. Another nine vessels were about twenty-four percent short of their full complements. If this experience were at all typical, royal ships needed a steady supply of recruits to keep the crews at strength. Official reports condemned certain irregularities in recruitment, such as the occasional use of force or the lack of a notary as the men were enrolled. At the same time, some officials argued for the recruitment of "vagabonds and petty criminals" (*vagamundos y rateros*) in order to get them off the streets; their recruitment was likely to be difficult without the use of force.

Outside Spain, royal officials in the 1730s relied on the lure of salary advances to fill the rosters. For example, in Naples naval gunners

---

[11]Henry Kamen, *The War of Succession in Spain, 1700-1715* (Bloomington, 1969), 58-59 and 140-141.

[12]Unless otherwise noted, the following discussion about registering mariners comes from AGS, Secretaría de Marina, legs. 276-277.

[13]University of Minnesota, James Ford Bell Library, Eugenio de Larruga, comp. "Historia de la Real y General Junta de Comercio," 12 vols. of compiled manuscripts and printed documents (Madrid, 1779-89), IX, fol. 202.

in 1734 received two gold doubloons to sign-up; able-bodied seamen and apprentices were offered 1.5 and one doubloon, respectively. Officials were assigned to specific districts to recruit mariners and filed separate reports for each. Within Spain, local officials were often assigned the task of recruiting mariners, but their sympathies lay more with the economic needs of the community than with the military needs of the crown. Officials in many coastal towns in Vizcaya and Guipúzcoa in 1734 argued that forced levies would ruin families, as well as the fishing and whaling industries upon which the community depended. Nonetheless, they did their duty by reporting on the men available and recruited them for royal service.[14] The lists that they provided indicate that the registration of mariners had begun in earnest by the early 1730s.

The official decree establishing marine registries ("*libros de matrícula*") was issued on 9 February 1737, as part of the reorganization of the navy and merchant marine. The overseeing agency was called the Admiralty (*Almirantazgo*), the culmination of ten years' work by José Patiño, who simultaneously ran the ministries of Marine and Indies, Finance, War, and State from 1726 to 1736. Like its prototypes in 1625 and 1726, the 1737 decree sought to create a registry for all of Spain's men of the sea (literally, *gente de mar*), forming them into "a separate and distinct guild with honours, exemptions, and privileges." The list would include mariners, artillerymen, carpenters and caulkers, as well as officers. Although explicitly aiming to foment commerce as well as the royal navy, the decree clearly placed the military foremost. All who registered were exempted from army levies and their permanent residences were excused from billeting troops. Any civil or criminal cases involving the registrants were thereafter to fall under the jurisdiction of Admiralty courts. The king invited foreign mariners of the Catholic faith to serve in the Spanish navy, offering them the same benefits as natives if they married in Spain and maintained their registration as mariners. When they were needed to man royal vessels, registrants would be paid the customary enlistment bonus, plus travelling expenses to their port of embarkation. Although registration was technically voluntary, the 1737 decree placed so many restrictions on maritime activities by non-registrants that it was effectively mandatory. Retirement age was sixty, and anyone who remained on the registry for thirty years without desertion could enjoy all the privileges of registration

---

[14]AGS, Secretaría de Marina, leg. 251.

during his retirement. Even those who served a shorter time could have many of the benefits, and exemplary service was to be rewarded whenever it occurred. The decree emphasized that, even though nobles were to be schooled especially as naval officers, they would not have a monopoly on the honours and rewards in royal service at sea.[15]

As a result of the 1737 decree and the registrations in the next few years, Spain's mariners were counted fairly accurately.[16] To facilitate the creation and maintenance of the registries, the coastal areas were divided into three administrative districts. The Department of Ferrol, named for a key port in Galicia, included the whole north and northwest coasts. The Department of Cartagena covered the Mediterranean coast north from that town to the French border. And the Department of Cádiz comprised Spain's southern Mediterranean coast and the Atlantic coast of Andalusia west of Gibraltar.

In the Ferrol district, Galicia alone contained about 120 ports along its rugged coastline. Initially, Galicia was credited with nearly 5700 mariners, but the number was later reduced to about 3300 after excluding farmers who used small boats to travel between villages but were not real mariners. Asturias added nearly 2000 to the northern total, and the area around Santander, called by its medieval title of the "Four Towns of the Sea," added about 1200. The Basque area of Vizcaya, with its capital at Bilbao, resisted registration at first, with local officials arguing that it violated ancient privileges. Eventually, however, they produced a clear account of the shipwrights and mariners in this traditional seafaring region, enumerating over 2000 men fit for service, a figure that royal officials suspected was too low. In Vizcaya, as in Galicia and other areas of the north, many men who were primarily farmers or craftsmen also knew how to handle small boats, but may have had experience in deep-sea sailing as well. Some Vizcayans may have avoided registration by falsely claiming that they were not primarily mariners. The other Basque area on the coast – Guipúzcoa, with its capital at San Sebastián – also delayed registering its mariners, and I was unable to find a count among the documents. Based on a levy for Vizcaya and Guipúzcoa in 1739, plus the figures available for Vizcaya,

---

[15]Larruga, "Historia," IX, fols. 202-209.

[16]Unless otherwise noted, the following discussion is based on documents in AGS, Secretaría de Marina, legs. 276-278.

I have estimated that Guipúzcoa had about 1500 mariners. In all, the Department of Ferrol contained 10,000 mariners about 1740. At the same time, I have estimated the total population of northern Spanish regions with coatlines at nearly 1.8 million. In other words, mariners accounted for about .6% of the northern population, though undoubtedly a much higher percentage of the coastal towns alone.

The Mediterranean coast northward from Cartagena registered over 14,000 mariners in the same period, more than half of them in Catalonia. The registries were particularly detailed in this district, differentiating among various specialties of shipwright as well as several categories of mariner. The total population of the Mediterranean coastal regions was nearly 1.8 million about 1740, so that mariners comprised about .8% of the eastern population. The resurgent economy in the early eighteenth century seems to have drawn more people to the coastal areas near Barcelona, while the inland areas grew less markedly.

Spain's southern coast contained a variety of diverse regions economically and demographically. The southeastern desert between Murcia and Almería held few people. Nor was the area favoured economically. By contrast, the Andalusian coasts in the southwest had been a hub of Spain's Atlantic fishing and commerce since the late Middle Ages, and the official base for Spain's American trade since the late fifteenth century. Most of the 13,000 mariners registered in the south about 1740 were concentrated from the Portuguese border to Tarifa near the Strait of Gibraltar; the rest lived in ports in the Málaga district. Mariners comprised slightly more of the total population in the south than they did in the east, about .84%. In Spain as a whole, registered mariners made up .74% of the population of the coastal provinces.

The number of mariners fit for service was somewhat smaller than the total number of registrants. There were no age limits for registration, and many ancient mariners signed up, presumably hoping for rewards for past service. The government evidently accomodated them. Retirees continued to receive benefits as long as they remained on the books, although it was unlikely that they would ever be called to serve again. Most of the available records note how many registrants were fit for service: in the north, seventy-five percent were; in the east, seventy-nine percent; and in the south, ninety-two percent – or about eighty-three percent overall. It is tempting to conclude from those figures that the sea-going population was younger in the south, but that is difficult to prove without information on the ages of all registrants.

Table 4
Estimates of Mariners by Coastal Region: Summary

Region	Maritime Area	Potential Mariners c. 1625?	Registered Mariners c. 1740	Percent fit for Service c. 1740	Coastal Population c. 1740	Percent Mariners c. 1740
Asturias	1	900	1,954	72.7		
Cantabria	1	1,350				
Galicia	1	6,600	3,343	75.1		
Guipuzcoa	1	900	1,500*			
Santander area	1		1,239	76.6		
Vizcaya	1	1,350	2,046			
Catalonia	2	4,500	7,641	76.3		
Mallorca	2	900	2,863	87.7		
Murcia	2	1,500	1,863	93.9		
Valencia	2	3,000	2,068	66.4		
Andalucia	3	4,500				
Ayamonte	3		1,844	88.5		
Cadiz	3		4,056	92.1		
Granada	3	4,500				
Malaga	3		2,353	93.4		
Puerto Real	3		2,775	91.4		
Sevilla	3		1,583	93.2		
Tarifa	3		481	100.0		
North Coast		11,100	10,082	74.7	1,759,000	0.57
East Coast		9,900	14,435	79.0	1,759,000	0.82
South Coast		9,000	13,092	92.0	1,566,000	0.84
Totals		30,000	37,609	83.3	5,084,000	0.74

Note: The figure for Guipúzcoa is estimated. North Coast = Area 1; East Coast = Area 2; and South Coast = Area 3.

Source: Archivo General de Simancas (AGS), Secretaría de Marina, legs. 276-278, for data on mariners. See table 1 for population.

The Demand for Mariners

Many scholars have tried to estimate the total shipping tonnage for various European countries in the early modern era. Some of the estimates are based on little more than unfounded assumptions or nationalistic prejudices. Others are based on solid documentation, such as the lists of ships in Spain's Indies trade. The House of Trade (*Casa de Contratación*) in Seville was founded in 1503 to administer shipping and trade with Spain's American colonies, long before the extent of the American lands was known. In the centuries that followed, the House of Trade kept continuous records of the merchantmen in the annual fleets and the military vessels that accompanied them. Many of the lists included the tonnage, as well as the owner, master, and various other officials on each ship. Pierre and Huguette Chaunu painstakingly analyzed the listings in the *Contratación* section of the Archive of the Indies in Seville and published their findings in a massive twelve volume set.[17] Although other scholars have found much to criticize in the Chaunus' data manipulations, nearly everyone uses the listings, grateful that someone else has done the work. In my judgment, the data are trustworthy for the number of ships and probably for the recorded tonnage.[18] Based on the data, we know that by the 1520s nearly 100 ships each year carried merchandise across the Atlantic between Spain and its American colonies. Together, the ships represented about 9000 *toneladas* of carrying capacity, each *tonelada* being equivalent to about 1.42 cubic meters. By the late sixteenth century, a yearly average of 150-200 ships was involved in the Indies trade, with a total tonnage of 30,000-40,000 *toneladas* (an average of 200 *toneladas* per ship). In other words, the number of ships and their average size had doubled since the

---

[17]Pierre Chaunu, with Huguette Chaunu, *Séville et l'Atlantique, 1504-1650* (8 vols. in 12, Paris, 1955-1960).

[18]The following discussion of ships and tonnage in the Indies trade is taken from my article, "The Growth and Composition of Trade in the Iberian Empires, 1450-1750," in James D. Tracy (ed.), *The Rise of Merchant Empires. Long-distance Trade in the Early Modern World, 1350-1750* (New York, 1990).

1520s, leading to a four-fold increase in carrying capacity.[19] For comparison, Fernand Braudel has estimated that there were about 350,000 tons of shipping in the Mediterranean in the late sixteenth century and 600,000-700,000 tons in the Atlantic for all maritime activities, including fishing, figures that would seem to overestimate the Mediterranean and underestimate the Atlantic for that period.[20]

In the late sixteenth and early seventeenth centuries, a guard squadron of six to eight galleons usually accompanied the fleet that headed toward the northern coast of South America (Tierra Firme). The fleet that served the eastern coast of Mexico (New Spain) had a smaller escort of two galleons. The convoy system and its military escorts had been developed in the early sixteenth century to thwart piracy, emanating largely from France and England, although the Dutch also preyed on Spanish merchantmen after 1568. Although the convoy system was not as all-inclusive as its planners intended, it still accounted for about eighty-five percent of the trade.

Sometime before the end of the sixteenth century the first long expansionary cycle of Spanish imperial trade approached its limits. The peak in shipping volume came in the quinquennium ending in 1610, after population, agriculture, and industry had already turned downward. Once trade declined, fleets sailed irregularly and the convoy system almost broke down. In the late 1620s, there were still nearly 120 ships per year in the Indies trade, with a cargo capacity of about 37,000 *toneladas*. By the late 1640s, however, an annual average of fewer than seventy-five ships carried the remaining trade, and from the late 1650s to the late 1660s, between thirty and thirty-five ships.[21] These figures changed little before a hiatus in the records from 1699 to 1717. Shipping volume was undoubtedly both minimal and sporadic during the first two decades

---

[19]Chaunu, with Chaunu, *Séville et l'Atlantique*, VI (1), 168 and 337. The authors (VI (1), 29-30) assumed that the definition of the Spanish *tonelada* changed over time and adjusted the tonnages in Spanish records to weighted figures (*unités pondérées*). Fortunately, they also printed the given tonnages, because other scholars have generally rejected their arguments about the *tonelada*.

[20]Fernand Braudel, *The Mediterranean and the Mediterranean World in the Age of Philip II* (2 vols., New York, 1972), I, 445-448.

[21]Chaunu, with Chaunu, *Séville et l'Atlantique*, VI (1), 168 and 337; Lutgardo García Fuentes, *Comercio español con América (1650-1700)* (Seville, 1980), 417-422.

of the new century, partly due to the War of the Spanish Succession. When the records resume, they show the start of a long-term recovery in the Indies trade, with fifty to sixty ships per year in the 1750s and more than 100 ships per year by the late 1770s, with an average size of over 400 *toneladas*. By the late eighteenth century, shipping volume was approaching its earlier peak volume.[22]

What proportion of Spain's total shipping tonnage did the Indies fleets represent? No one knows. In a classic 1932 article, Abbott Payson Usher estimated that they amounted to about one-tenth around 1585, which in his calculations meant a total of about 200,000 *toneladas* for Spanish merchant shipping as a whole. Usher then retreated from his own conclusion and lowered the estimate to somewhere between 150,000 and 175,000 *toneladas*.[23] Most subsequent scholars have accepted that global figure, although they vary in their use of related data from Usher, the Chaunus, and others.[24] For the sake of argument, let us assume that Usher was correct in thinking that the Indies fleets comprised one-tenth of Spain's total merchant shipping. Based on the Chaunus' figures, Indies shipping from 1585 to its peak in 1610 averaged 170 ships and more than 38,000 *toneladas* per year. Total merchant shipping would have been over 380,000 *toneladas*, probably too high but not unbelievable.

The Spanish crown rented merchant vessels to serve in naval fleets during wartime, but it retained a core of vessels for escort and defense even during peacetime. How much did naval vessels add to Spain's total shipping tonnage? Again, no one knows. The official Spanish summary of the fleet sent against England in 1588 included 130 vessels of 57,868 *toneladas*. Nine of the twenty largest vessels were

---

[22] Antonio García-Baquero González, *Cádiz y el Atlántico (1717-1778)* (2 vols., Cádiz, 1976), II, 123-137.

[23] One suspects, though it is impossible to prove, that he revised his estimate downward largely because his higher figure would have put Spain above the Netherlands, an unthinkable notion to most European economic historians, then and now. Abbott Payson Usher, "Spanish Ships and Shipping in the Sixteenth and Seventeenth Centuries," in *Facts and Factors in Economic History: For Edwin Francis Gay* (Cambridge, MA, 1932), 211-212.

[24] See, for example, Richard W. Unger, "The Tonnage of Europe's Merchant Fleets, 1300-1800," *American Neptune*, LII (Fall 1992). Unfortunately, Unger (p. 256) adopts the Chaunus' mistaken notion of the size of the *tonelada* and hence underestimates the size of the average ship in the Indies trade by about half.

Spanish warships, totalling about 5100 *toneladas*. Many ships in the Spanish fleet were merchantmen (*naos*), and over half the tonnage was foreign-built, mostly chartered by the crown. In all, there were 29,453 men in the fleet, 8050 of whom were sailors.[25] That works out to a manning ratio of about one sailor for every seven *toneladas*, fairly typical for a Spanish war fleet. In 1634, the Armada del Mar Océano (Atlantic Fleet) alone had thirty-three warships (probably about 15,000 *toneladas*), but two years later, it was thought to need 30,000 *toneladas* because France had entered the Thirty Years' War as an enemy.[26]

The manning ratio for Spanish ships varied considerably, with one man for every five to ten *toneladas*, depending on the type of ship and the purpose of the voyage. Merchant vessels had to carry sufficient crew to defend against enemies and pirates, even when they did not carry infantry regiments. Thus, Spanish manning ratios were much higher than, for example, those of Dutch merchantmen in the Baltic. Some authors avoid the concept of manning ratios altogether, because the magnitude of the *tonelada* has been in dispute. Nonetheless, manning ratios make the data for Spain roughly comparable to that of other European countries. Enough work has been done on the *tonelada* to assign it the plausible size of 1.42 cubic meters, about the same as the old sea ton (*tonneau de mer*) of Bordeaux, and to argue that it retained that value for the whole of the early modern period.[27]

We can arbitrarily estimate a range for the number of sailors required for Spain's total shipping based on the data discussed thus far. First, assume that total merchant shipping fell somewhere within the range of eight to ten times that of shipping in the Indies trade. Second, assume that naval ships added another 30,000 *toneladas* in normal years (when a major fleet was not planned but when Spain still had to defend

---

[25]Colin Martin and Geoffrey Parker, *La Gran Armada* (Madrid, 1988), 61-62, reproduces the official spreadsheet summarizing the fleet. José Luis Casado Soto, *Los barcos españoles del siglo XVI y la Gran Armada de 1588* (Madrid, 1988), 186-226, analyzes the Spanish fleet in detail and adjusts the official figures somewhat.

[26]Carla Rahn Phillips, *Six Galleons for the King of Spain: Imperial Defense in the Early Seventeenth Century* (Baltimore, 1986), 201-202.

[27]Michel Morineau, *Jauge et méthodes de jauge anciennes et modernes* (Paris, 1966), 31-34, 64 and 115-116, has argued persuasively that the *tonelada* equalled 1.42 cubic metres.

its fleets and coasts). Then, apply the ratios of one man for every eight to ten *toneladas* for merchant shipping, and one man for every six to seven *toneladas* for naval vessels. While much of this reasoning is speculative, it at least provides an order of magnitude for the demand for sailors. At the minimum multiplier for merchant shipping (eight times the Indies trade), and the minimum manning ratio (one for every ten *toneladas*), merchant shipping would have required over 36,000 men at the turn of the seventeenth century, when the Indies trade peaked.[28] Naval needs would have raised the total to over 40,000 men. According to the estimate that is associated with papers from 1625, Spain then had about 30,000 mariners, at a point when the slump in population and trade was well under way. Thereafter, the continuing depression reduced the overall demand for mariners. The Thirty Years' War, which was very destructive of human lives and property, nonetheless provided employment for mariners. In about 1740, with the revival of trade and continuing military needs, Spain again would have needed 35,000-40,000 men. The detailed lists for 1737-1739 included nearly 38,000 men, of whom about 32,000 were fit for service. In other words, if my calculations approximate reality, Spain's maritime population fell short of the demand most of the time during the early modern period, and it fell far short in certain circumstances, especially when the needs of trade and warfare expanded at the same time.

A Shortage of Mariners?

Based on complaints in the documentary record, it seems that shortages of qualified mariners were chronic from the late sixteenth century, yet the causes remain in dispute. Contemporaries often noted the low status of sailors in a society that accorded more respect to soldiers. One suspects that these status distinctions sprang from the natural antagonism between the inland areas, which held the bulk of the population, and the coastal zones, which held a small proportion of total population but virtually all the mariners. By and large, early modern Spain identified with the settled agricultural life of inland Castile. Many Spaniards

---

[28]Pérez-Mallaína, *Hombres del océano*, 57-59, eschews manning ratios in favour of a ratio of men per vessel, based on several lists of important ships in the Indies trade. He estimates a need for 7000-9000 mariners during the peak of the Indies trade, which seems high but may be plausible.

considered sailors to be vile and despised the unsettled lifestyle that characterized seafaring. Distinguished mariners from noble families with a tradition of seafaring could ignore such prejudices, but ordinary mariners could not. The low status might have depressed the supply of mariners over the long term. Diego Brochero, a nobleman expert in Spanish military affairs in the early seventeenth century, argued that the best sailors switched to soldiering if they had career ambitions in the military. Or they sailed with fishing and merchant fleets rather than with armadas because they were treated better in the absence of soldiers.[29]

Some contemporaries blamed low pay for the chronic shortage of skilled mariners, especially on naval vessels. There is little question that maritime wages were low and that military stipends were lower than those on merchantmen, although there is some difficulty in quantifying and tracing those wages over time. The crown paid wages by the month from the early sixteenth century, in addition to providing food, drink, and housing (such as it was) for the duration of a voyage. Merchant ships had various modes of payment, from shares of the profits or merchandise of a voyage to a flat salary.[30] In the early days of Spanish exploration, the "shares" of a voyage were often much more valuable than the wages. Merchant vessels also provided lodging and sustenance. On both military and merchant voyages, sailors customarily received an advance on their wages when they enlisted. The amount varied with the difficulty, length, or danger of the voyage and could be as high as six months' or a year's salary. Normal voyages of warships customarily paid two months' wages in advance, and merchant ships paid ten to twenty percent of the agreed round-trip salary. Sailors on voyages to the Indies supplemented their wages by taking clothes or other merchandise to sell. So did commanders, sometimes even the most distinguished ones.

Wages on military vessels fell far short of wages for many other occupations in late sixteenth-century Spain. Summary information provided by Pablo Emilio Pérez-Mallaína makes the point clearly. The figures are given in *maravedís* (mrs).

---

[29]AGS, Guerra Antigua, leg. 3152, memoranda of April and May 1628.

[30]A thorough and thoughtful discussion of mariners' wages is included in Pérez-Mallaína, *Hombres del océano*, 102-117.

Year	Armada Sailor wage + ration	Carpenters, caulkers and masons in Seville	Workers in inland Castile
1500-33	35-45 mrs/day	55-85 mrs/day	22-35 mrs
1534-66	45-65 mrs/day	85-204	35-68
1567-1600	65-100	204-306	68-85

The wages of others on board were related proportionately. Pages made half a sailor's wage, pilots and masters made twice as much, and the wages of minor officers and gunners ranged in between. The value of rations was the same for all, figured at thirty-four maravedís per day in 1566 and fifty in 1600. According to Pérez-Mallaína's figures, the wage gap widened during the sixteenth century between specialized workers in Seville and mariners on military vessels. Prices rose five-fold during the sixteenth century; although the wages of specialized land workers did not match inflation, they came closer than those of either sailors on naval vessels or workers in inland Castile. Inland workers briefly made more than sailors at mid-century, before the crown raised sailors' wages and inland workers again fell behind. Judging from the prices for a variety of foods in the late sixteenth century, an unmarried sailor who saved his salary for the duration of an eight-month voyage could afford to eat well for the rest of the year. Yet his salary did not suffice to feed a family without supplementary income.[31]

Merchant marine wages are more difficult to figure, but a variety of evidence suggests they were consistently higher than on naval vessels. Because many seamen signed-on as a way of emigrating to the Indies, desertions were high once the ships reached their destination. Masters often had to pay premiums to find crews for the return voyage. Wages alone in the last third of the sixteenth century, not including the value of rations, showed the following range:

Destination	Spain-America-Spain	America-Spain
New Spain	50-60 ducats, or 18,750-22,500 maravedís	25-65 ducats, or 9,375-24,375 maravedís
Tierra Firme	50-104 ducats, or 18,750-39,000 maravedís	40-60 ducats, or 15,000-22,500 maravedís

---

[31]*Ibid.*, 117-118.

The most common wage for the New Spain voyage was sixty ducats. With an average of eight months for the round trip, wages on merchantmen were the equivalent of 2800 *maravedís* per month, compared to 1500 *maravedís* per month on naval ships, plus rations in both cases. Merchant voyages to Tierra Firme paid a bit more than those to New Spain, and some sailors earned a huge salary for the return trip to Spain. A merchant mariner could feed a family on his annual wage of fifty to sixty ducats, especially since his own food and drink were provided for eight months. By comparison, average income in the inland areas of Castile in the mid-1570s was forty-four ducats per year, and the wage earner had to feed himself as well as his family.[32] With a fairly low salary and little chance to save, most mariners were poor, just barely making a living if they did not rise through the ranks or supplement their income through trade or other means. And mariners on naval vessels were much worse off than their counterparts on merchantmen.

Why were wages so low on naval vessels, especially since many contemporaries complained about a shortage of skilled mariners? Some observers claimed that if the crown raised wages on naval ships, crews could be levied more easily, which implied that the shortage was not absolute but relative to the wage level. That was a logical assessment of the situation, but it was not likely to be acted upon. Maritime wage levels remained low, relying on the ready pool of labour on the coasts. The coastal areas were not favoured agricultural zones and the local population depended on the sea for employment and occasional imports of basic foodstuffs. Though some mariners undoubtedly engaged in other employment for part of their adult lives, there does not seem to have been any serious competition for their services in agriculture, industry, mining, or other local occupations before industrialization. The diversity of occupations on the coasts, including seafaring, sustained a population that grew moderately during the early modern period, but without encouraging a rapid population rise that would have greatly depressed maritime wages and without precipitating a sharp decline in population that would have driven wages upward. The situation discouraged many Spaniards from serving on royal ships, whose dangerous missions made seafaring even less attractive. In the Basque region, by the late sixteenth century commentators noted with alarm that young men preferred to

---

[32]*Ibid.*, 120-123. The author does not mention the cost of food for the inland worker.

concentrate on fishing rather than sail for the crown as their ancestors had done.

Perhaps as important in keeping maritime wages low was the availability of foreigners to supplement Spain's internal supply. Foreigners worked on Spanish vessels throughout the early modern era, and their presence was especially notable when one of them commanded a vessel or fleet, as in the 1519 expedition under Ferdinand Magellan. In 1568 the House of Trade limited foreigners to six per ship for security reasons, or about twelve to fifteen percent of the crew. Yet even on important naval voyages, foreigners often accounted for twenty percent or more of the crew, and often a third of the gunners. Foreign sailors filled the gap between demand and supply in Spain as they did elsewhere.[33] About fifty percent of the foreigners were from Portugal, twenty-five percent were Italian, and the rest were divided among "Levantiscos" from various parts of the eastern Mediterranean, plus Flemings and Germans. Not surprisingly, very few were English or French, Spain's habitual enemies in the early modern period. By contrast, only about four percent of the infantry carried on Spanish warships was foreign.[34] Perhaps because of the higher status of soldiers, Spaniards seem to have found infantry service much more attractive than work as sailors.

Many foreigners undoubtedly joined as mariners to enter the Spanish Indies, knowing that it was nearly impossible for non-Spaniards to obtain a license to immigrate. Others were simply looking for work unavailable at home or unavailable at similar wage levels. Foreigners could pass as Spaniards fairly easily because of the linguistic variations in Spain. They also benefitted from the willing cooperation of masters and even royal officials, whose most important goal was to fill the crew, even if that meant disobeying official rules on foreign mariners. Foreigners were often willing to accept minimal pay, short rations, and brutal conditions to avoid detection. From the perspective of merchant masters in particular, they made ideal seamen. The net result was to expand the labour pool and dampen pressure on wages, even in situations of rising demand. After nearly two centuries of trying to enforce quotas

---

[33]England also had trouble meeting its needs for crews as its seafaring prominence increased. See Christopher Lloyd, *The British Seamen, 1200-1860. A Social Survey* (London, 1968).

[34]Pérez-Mallaína, *Hombres del océano*, 63-64.

on foreigners, the crown explicitly recognized their value in the decree setting up the mariners' registry in 1737. Although foreigners had to meet several requirements in order to gain full benefits, the decree marked official recognition of the reality of maritime recruitment.

Over the whole of the early modern period, a market for maritime labour functioned in Spain. For merchant voyages and even for military service, officials relied on recruitment much more than forced levies to make up crews. Although these conditions would seem to have allowed the market to determine wage rates and to influence the supply of mariners, other conditions combined to blunt its effect. The weak agricultural and manufacturing base in the coastal areas provided little competition for maritime occupations and tended to hold wages down. The availability of foreigners further dampened the bargaining power of skilled maritime labour. Mariners' wages rose in times of increasing demand, but not as far as they might have. And military service, which habitually paid less than merchant labour, could turn to forced levies in times of crisis, generally avoiding the need to raise wages to competitive levels.

Recruitment and Promotion:
The Merchant Fleet of Salem, Massachusetts, 1670-1765

Vince Walsh

In *Mariners and Markets*, Charles Kindleberger asks if labour markets for mariners in the age of sail were efficient.[1] He defined efficiency by borrowing three neo-classical concepts. First, a market is efficient if it allows free access for both employers and labour. Second, it is efficient if it clears – that is, if demand for labour induces a corresponding supply (from outside the area, if necessary) or leads to an increase in wages. Third, it is efficient if labour commands the same price throughout the market. Kindleberger was unclear whether any one or all of these criteria were required for a market to be efficient. But he argues that to test for efficiency certain key topics must be examined: recruitment and pay; the treatment of seamen at sea and on shore; and the level of government intervention into markets.

This essay focuses on recruitment and asks if labour and management had free access to each other. Using the maritime labour market in Salem, Massachusetts from 1670 to the eve of the American Revolution, I intend to show that from the turn of the century to 1775 the majority of mariners who sailed in Salem-owned vessels were recruited from within the town; few came from the countryside and even fewer from outside the colony. Such a market existed because of several positive attractions offered by a career at sea. First, any recruit had a good chance of promotion to master or mate. Second, little economic or social distance existed between the master and the recruit. A Salem mariner often came from a similar social and economic background, frequently grew up and lived in the same neighbourhood, and usually knew a master and his reputation before ever sailing under him. Third, early in the eighteenth century a tradition of seafaring developed in many Salem

---

[1]Charles P. Kindleberger, *Mariners and Markets* (New York, 1992).

families, with a son following in the footsteps of his father or uncle. Although not all mariners were recruited from such families, a significant number were. Finally, an important social division helped define the Salem market. Because of paternal and fraternal links between master and crew, social divisions cut vertically along community lines, centring on whether a mariner was a resident or a stranger.

Mariners were identified from the business accounts of several Salem shipowners between 1667 and 1765.[2] One of the most valuable items in such accounts were the portledge bills, which listed the name, rank, length of employment, and monthly wage of each crew member, as well as the origin and destination of the voyage.[3] Both the residence and socio-economic status of masters and seamen were derived from the Salem tax lists, which listed the levies paid by the head of every household in 1683 and annually from 1689 to 1771. When a mariner's name was not listed in the records, the genealogical footnotes in Sidney Perley's *The History of Salem, Massachusetts* were consulted to determine whether or not he belonged to the town.[4]

Salem was the most important town and port in Essex County during the period. Originally settled by people who socially and economically belonged to the middling ranks of English society, these generally prosperous and independent souls brought to New England a strong Puritan ethic, including the ideas that the family was the basic

---

[2]The family papers and account books of six merchant shipowners were examined. They were the George Corwin Account Books (1658-1664, 1663-1672) and Curwin Family Papers (1641-1902); English/Touzel/Hathorne Papers (1661-1851); Timothy Orne Family Papers and Accounts (1719-1899); Miles Ward Family Papers and Accounts (1718-1945); Richard Derby Family Papers and Accounts (1757-1776), and the Goodhue Family Papers (1762). All are housed in the James Duncan Phillips Library, Peabody Essex Museum, Salem, MA.

[3]A portledge bill was a claim for the crew's wages submitted by the master to the vessel's owner(s). Although "portledge" was the usual spelling in Massachusetts, it was sometimes spelled "portlidge," "portledg," or "portlage." In England it was usually spelled "portage" and originally referred to the "portage" or cargo a crew member was allowed to take on a voyage. With time, however, it came to refer to the crew's claims for wages and allowances.

[4]Sidney Perley, *The History of Salem, Massachusetts* (3 vols., Salem, 1924), is invaluable for any historian attempting to identify or trace Salem families. It was also the most important source used here to examine inter-generational maritime traditions.

societal unit; that the head of each household was responsible for its protection and spiritual growth; and that a degree of independence was needed to maintain and manifest a covenant with God.[5] Independence was largely defined by land, and the aim of the founders was to grant to each church member sufficient acreage to assure it. Yet the Puritans also believed in a hierarchical society which, as in England, was defined by landed wealth. The amount of land owned both determined and reflected the owner's wealth and status of Salem's original settlers.[6]

Despite economic growth, the colony continued to be dependent upon England for many consumer goods. That it had few wares to trade created a balance of payments problem, the solution to which changed and ultimately undermined the Puritan aristocracy. For the first eleven years of its existence, Massachusetts was able to cover its debts with funds brought in by newcomers. In 1640 civil war broke out in England, abruptly halting the flow of immigrants and creating a payments crisis. Yet by diminishing the Newfoundland fishery, the war also created an opportunity and New Englanders, including residents of Salem, began to catch cod and market it in southern Europe, filling the void left by the English. With markets in the West Indies also expanding, fish and timber became important exports. At first these goods were carried in English ships, but local people soon began to construct their own; coastal New England, including Salem, entered the maritime world.[7]

The Puritan landed gentry constituted Salem's leadership for its first twenty years. But in the 1650s, as the mercantile sector began to grow in wealth and prominence, tension between the old leadership and the merchants on the harbour front emerged. It finally reached a crisis in the early 1680s and was defused only when the merchants wrested control of town affairs from the original leaders.[8] There were several reasons for this tension and the eventual leadership upheaval. First, most

---

[5]Much of the following discussion is taken from Richard P. Gildrie, *Salem, Massachusetts 1626-1683: A Covenant Community* (Charlottesville, VA, 1975); and Bernard Bailyn, *The New England Merchants in the Seventeenth Century* (New York, 1964).

[6]Gildrie, *Salem*, 70.

[7]Bailyn, *New England Merchants*, 75-86.

[8]*Ibid.*, 134-141.

merchants were not original settlers, and since some did not wish to become church members, their presence and wealth began to upset the community's economic and social equilibrium. Although this was not overly serious in the beginning, when the majority of merchants who became community leaders also became church members, over time fewer joined the church and even those who did looked upon membership more in conceptual than religious terms. Where religious conviction and the conversion experience were central to the original settlers, they were often absent from the lives of later merchants. Second, because the majority of new immigrants of lower social and economic levels did not join the church, church members became a minority. Third, the town eventually ran out of land. New immigrants could not achieve the degree of independence that had been envisioned originally. As wage labourers, they did not share the same loyalties to Puritan ideals as did independent farmers. Finally, Puritanism's energy, undermined by the restoration of Charles II in 1660, was withering in Salem by the 1680s.

Salem merchants began to see status and wealth as things to be pursued for their own sake. Where the original leaders led frugal lives despite their wealth, the new leadership was more ostentatious. More important, mercantile wealth quickly outstripped landed affluence. Where the richest farming estate of 1681 was appraised at £800, the wealthiest merchant in town by 1684 left an estate of £5000, and at the turn of the century one merchant left over £30,000. The holders of this new wealth did not consciously conspire to overthrow the establishment: merchants simply had different goals. As a result, Salem in 1640 began the transition from farming to a seaport town, a shift that was completed by the early 1680s. Salem became and remained a haven for merchants, artisans and mariners throughout the colonial period.[9]

---

[9]*Ibid.*, 83 and 168; Gildrie, *Salem*, 155-169; and James G. Lydon, "Fish for Gold: The Massachusetts Fish Trade with Iberia, 1700-1773," *New England Quarterly*, LIV (1981), 539-582. Salem followed a different developmental route than other Puritan towns. While many interior farming communities remained faithful to Puritan ideals well into the eighteenth century, trade changed the players who occupied the pinnacle of the socio-economic order in ports. Salem (and also Boston) was one of the first towns in which the landed gentry lost control. Although the passion for Puritan ideals withered, this does not imply that pre-industrial paternal and fraternal relationships died. In fact, I will show later that such relationships played an important role in recruitment. For a variety of viewpoints on the development of New England towns, see Christine Heyrman, *Commerce and Culture: The Maritime Communities of Colonial Massachusetts 1690-1750* (New York, 1984); Byron Fairchild, *Messrs. William Pepperrell, Merchants*

During the early years of Salem's maritime development its mariners alternated between fishing as far north as Sable Island and shipping goods along the Atlantic coast. The first traders serviced the fishery and from 1640 sent their vessels as far as Newfoundland. The town's maritime experience grew out of the fishery, and it was from that involvement that its growing fleet of small ketches ventured into shipping. This early shift resulted from the opportunity for Salem fishing vessels to serve the growing communities along the Massachusetts coast, especially north of Salem, on their way to and from the fishing grounds. Bringing supplies to these communities and carrying to Salem or Boston the fish and other commodities these towns produced became a routine activity. Indeed, some of the ketches were soon used to carry fish outside the colony. Although a clearer distinction between a fishing skipper and a shipping master emerged over time, it was common throughout the colonial period for a skipper to fish in the warm months and to make a winter voyage with a cargo of fish and lumber, sometimes to southern Europe or more frequently to the West Indies.[10]

Until 1660 Salem vessels most frequently traded with the northern colonies, but they soon sailed farther south. Their first ports of call were in Maryland and Virginia, where they sold supplies to plantations and loaded tobacco for Britain. Once this route was established the southern colonies became for a time their most important destination. There were direct voyages to Britain as early as 1651, but this route never became important for the town. Nor, in fact, did the trade with southern Europe. Although some fish assembled in Salem for shipment to Spain and Portugal was carried by Salem vessels, most went in craft belonging to Boston or British owners. While later in the century

---

at Piscataqua (Ithaca, NY, 1954); Philip Greven, *Four Generations: Population, Land and Family in Colonial Andover, Massachusetts* (Ithaca, NY, 1970); Stephen Innes, *Labour in a New Land: Economy and Society in Seventeenth-Century Springfield* (Princeton, 1983); Christopher M. Jedrey, *The World of John Cleaveland: Family and Community in Eighteenth-Century New England* (New York, 1979); and Darrett Rutman, *Winthrop's Boston: Portrait of a Puritan Town, 1630-1649* (New York, 1965).

[10]Small vessels specializing in carrying goods along the coast also appeared. The men who handled such craft became known simply as "coasters". Interestingly, most of these vessels and crews came not from Salem but from northern communities. In the Essex Quarterly Court records, Newbury and Ipswich were most frequently mentioned as the residences of coasting masters.

Salem began carrying a greater share of this trade, it was another fifty years before this became a majority.[11]

By the late 1660s Salem vessels regularly visited the West Indies, and these voyages increased over the next ten years as the wealth of the sugar islands grew. Although in the 1670s this trade was not nearly as important as coastal commerce, by 1680 the West Indies became the most popular destination for Salem vessels, a fact that remained true to the end of the colonial era.[12] By the last decade of the seventeenth century the town's major trade routes had been established; despite the many wars of the next eighty years, they remained virtually unchanged.

It appears that almost from the beginning the mariners who manned Salem's vessels resided in the town. Although data on recruitment are fragmentary before the end of Queen Anne's War, an examination of the account books of Salem shipowners and merchants tends to support this. For example, over two-thirds of the mariners listed in the Corwin account books from 1667 to 1678 lived in Salem for most if not all of their lives.[13] The majority of crew aboard Salem vessels listed in the Essex County notarial records from 1689 to 1709 were residents.[14]

---

[11]James G. Lydon, "North Shore Trade in the Early Eighteenth Century," *American Neptune*, XXVIII (1968), 261-274.

[12]The sources for these voyages include the account books of Salem merchants and their business letters; Massachusetts customs records; Essex County court records; and Massachusetts notarial records. Notarial records were special statements made by masters, usually listing damages to a ship or cargo due to natural causes. It was a form of protection against being held responsible for the cost of repairs. The destinations listed in the portledge bills also reinforce the argument that Salem vessels visited the West Indies most frequently: of fifty destinations given between 1711 and 1770, one was in northern Europe, three in the northern colonies, six in southern Europe (including Madeira), seventeen in Virginia or Maryland, and twenty-three in the West Indies.

[13]George Corwin was one of Salem's most prominent merchants during the last quarter of the seventeenth century. His accounts listed the names of twenty-six mariners who sailed in his vessels from 1667 to 1678. Of these, sixteen lived in Salem, four had settled in neighbouring Beverly and Marblehead (and three others likely lived there), one resided in Ipswich, one in Lynn, and the residence of one was unknown. Of the sixteen who settled in Salem, seven lived there for at least twenty years and four for at least ten. Of the five who stayed under ten years, three died while still residents.

[14]See "Essex County Notarial Records," *Essex Institute Historical Collections*, XLI (1905), 183-192, 381-398; XLII (1906), 153-168, 245-256.

From 1711 to 1765 over three-quarters of those listed in the portledge bills lived in the town. Significantly, almost seventy percent of those who did not, came from neighbouring coastal towns in Essex County. Fewer than ten percent were untraceable.[15]

Although the great majority of sailors from 1640 to 1690 were residents, only a minority belonged to the original settlement or were the heirs of those who did. Because of the Puritan emphasis on independence, and its association with land, shipowners had a difficult time attracting these men to a career at sea. For most Puritans, going to sea was alien and for some it was tantamount to living among the damned. Most mariners were therefore recent immigrants. For example, all but one of the crew listed in Corwin's accounts were first-generation residents and most arrived shortly before signing on. Among masters, however, a much higher percentage were original settlers or their heirs. Although still a minority, they comprised over forty percent of the total, which suggests that when possible Salem shipowners before 1690 promoted local men. It will be shown later that this policy continued throughout the colonial period.

After 1690 the industry was able to recruit substantially more local men.[16] The sources reveal that the majority of Salem seamen after

---

[15] In all, the names of 369 men were found in the portledge bills from 1711 to 1765. Their residences were determined by examining the Salem tax lists from 1710 to 1770, the Beverly and Marblehead tax lists from 1735 to 1772, the Massachusetts Tax Valuation Lists of 1771, and the Essex County Probate Index, which lists all registered probates in Essex county throughout the seventeenth, eighteenth, and nineteenth centuries. This index gives the name, death date, hometown, and occupation of the deceased. See Melinde Lutz Sanborn (ed.), *Essex County, Massachusetts, Probate Index, 1638-1840* (2 vols., Boston, 1987).

[16] From 1694 to 1720 the proportion of immigrant masters dropped dramatically to under thirty percent, and from 1720 to the end of the colonial period averaged around a third. In the portledge bills from 1724 to 1765 fifty-seven masters were listed. Of these thirty-seven (sixty-five percent) were at least second-generation residents of the town. In addition, where the majority of immigrant shipmasters before 1690 came from overseas, almost all post-1690 immigrant shipmasters came from neighbouring communities along the Massachusetts coast. It may be more accurate to argue that first-generation Salem masters were in the majority before 1690 and second- and later-generation masters comprised the bulk after 1694. From 1690 until 1694 there was a remarkable drop in the number of recorded voyages by Salem masters. Where the number from 1680 to 1684 and 1685 to 1689 had been seventy-nine and seventy voyages, respectively, the number from 1690 to 1694 dropped to thirty-one. More important, from the beginning of 1692

the turn of the century were single, young, and lived with parents or other guardians. Although any male over the age of sixteen of sound mind and body was charged a poll tax, it was normal for the head of the household to pay it for any son living at home. The father's poll tax, for example, would comprise payment for an extra head or two. Most Salem mariners below the level of mate had their taxes paid by a parent. Not until he married and headed a household was a son normally found on the tax lists, and this was usually several years after first appearing on a portledge bill; it was the rare seaman who earlier paid any personal or real estate taxes. Normally, while he remained single he lived at home and his parents received his wages, limiting his ability to accumulate savings or property. At times, it was explicitly stated in the portledge bill that wages were to be paid to a father or to the mother if a widow. In the case of a widow, who was exempt from the poll tax, the list might state that she paid the tax for her son. The responsibility of contributing to the family welfare obviously influenced the decision of when to marry. On average, Salem seamen did not wed until their mid-twenties.[17]

Many of these men went on to become masters and mates (a subject discussed below), but for those who did not their appearance on the tax lists often did not occur until they had disappeared from the portledge bills. In these cases men went to sea for several years and then returned to work ashore. Some decided they did not like the sea or were frustrated in their hopes for promotion, while others went to sea with the

---

to the end of 1694 only seven voyages were found. The lack of data may have been due to the fact that the voyages for these years were not recorded or their records lost. But I suspect that other factors played a significant role. Massachusetts had been involved in the disastrous invasion of French Canada in 1690; the enormous taxes levied in 1690 and 1691 to pay for this war (the rate for 1690 was nearly five times the 1689 level) must have seriously depressed the colony's trade for the next several years. Following this disaster, the 1692 witch trials decimated the town. The tax lists from the fall of that year show that almost half the citizenry, including large numbers of merchants and masters, had either fled or were unable to pay. Many of these families did not appear on the lists until 1694 while others never returned. Although the merchant community gained control of the town's political structure in the 1680s, it appears that it was not until after 1692 that the new leadership was able to solidify its victory. Considering that Britain was at war until 1697, a return to more normal trade followed 1694. From 1695 to 1699 sixty-nine voyages were recorded.

[17]The average marrying age of sixty-seven mariners from the portledge bills was 24.9 years.

intention of leaving after several years. Whatever the reason, it appears many stayed ashore after marriage. What they did on land is not at the moment clear but once they appeared in the tax lists they continued to appear for years afterwards.[18] The majority were the sons of Salem residents, and even most of those of unknown origin continued to dwell in the port and pay taxes.[19] Few had rural roots. The majority grew up in an urban world; if only a few came from the colony's farms, still fewer returned there. The Salem tax lists were divided into wards and until 1752 the area that became the farming community of Danvers comprised four of the eight wards. Yet from 1683 until 1752 only four mariners came from this area. All other mariners who lived in Salem, regardless of generation, came from the four urban wards. And all non-Salem mariners whose home towns were traceable came from the ports of Massachusetts.

The great majority of vessels clearing from Salem over the period were ketches, sloops or schooners, usually of between thirty-five and forty tons burthen.[20] Such craft did not permit much physical separation of the master from the crew; moreover, because much work was shared, there could be little social distance. Each vessel usually included a master, mate, boy, and two or three seamen. With a crew of five, the master and a seaman often handled one watch and the mate and

---

[18]An extensive database is currently in the process of being created at Memorial University of Newfoundland by my distinguished colleague, Daniel Vickers, to address this and other questions. Thus far over 5000 New England seaman have been listed between 1640 to 1850.

[19]A random sample of 160 Salem resident mariners was taken for the period 1710-1760; of these only eighteen appeared in the tax lists for fewer than five years.

[20]The seventeenth-century Massachusetts ketch was a small two-masted vessel with a covered deck, almost always under fifty tons and manned by a crew of four to six, including the captain. Throughout the century it was the most common vessel used for trading along the coast and with the West Indies and was even used on trans-Atlantic crossings. It remained the vessel of choice until the end of Queen Anne's War in 1713, by which time the sloop and schooner had overtaken it. The crew size in the portledge bills ranged from four to eleven, depending on destination. Vessels bound for the northern colonies were smaller and carried crews of four to six. Those going to the southern colonies usually carried a crew of five, while those headed for the West Indies had six or seven mariners. The largest crews were on those vessels bound for northern or southern Europe that carried anywhere from eight to eleven mariners. The fifty voyages in the accounts had an average crew size of 6.2.

the second seaman the other. Such a small crew must have required the master to participate in some of the manual tasks, such as handling the wheel or making adjustments to the sails. This type of relationship came very close to that which Eric Sager asserts existed on early nineteenth-century Atlantic Canadian and Newfoundland schooners.[21] Concerning the boat fishery, Sager argues that there was an "ethic of egalitarian relations" in which the skipper was merely a man of seniority and experience working with close relations; decisions about how, where and when to fish depended upon group consensus rather than imposed authority. The result was that "every Bank fishing schooner was a sort of seafaring democracy." The masters and officers did not appropriate exclusive knowledge and an experienced deckhand on one voyage often showed up as master on the next. In addition, Sager contends that the coastal schooner shared some of this egalitarianism. On most passages seamen knew each other and the master. But paternalism, he argued, was more common than kinship.[22]

A similar relationship existed aboard Salem's fishing and merchant vessels. Even young men serving for the first time took with them knowledge and lore about the sea. These men grew up along the town's waterfront and smelled the saltfish on the wind from Winter Island or as it lay on the docks. They listened daily to tales of their fathers, uncles, older brothers, or neighbours; became familiar with many of the ropes and lines; and heard talk on the best and safest way to get to any port frequented by Salem vessels. More important, they grew up in the same neighbourhoods as the masters under whom they would one day sail and each knew (or knew of) the other. These close connections are again reflected in the tax lists. Almost without exception Salem masters and mariners came from one of the four urban wards. More telling, almost fifty percent of the seamen whose wards we know sailed with a master from the same ward. On some voyages every Salem crew member came from the same ward as the master.

---

[21]See Eric W. Sager, *Seafaring Labour: The Merchant Marine of Atlantic Canada, 1820-1914* (Montréal, 1989). Basil Greenhill, *The Merchant Schooners* (Annapolis, MD, 1988), argued that similar relationships existed among late nineteenth- and early twentieth-century British schooner men.

[22]Sager, *Seafaring Labour*, 47-52. By this he meant that because pre-industrial mercantile society was defined by master-servant relationships, these carried over onto such vessels.

The fraternal relationships between master and crew were most apparent on fishing voyages. An examination of the account books of fish merchants and owners of fishing vessels demonstrates this clearly. On Salem vessels fishing off the coast or on the Grand Banks the master received the same share as the other full sharemen. Nothing else appeared on the credit side of the master's account or on the debit side of the vessel's account to indicate otherwise. Further, a shareman on one voyage might show up as master on another. Not only did this demonstrate the existence of fraternal relationships, it also reveals that the art of navigation was not the exclusive preserve of the master and that any full shareman was capable of navigating.[23] How much of this knowledge was transferred from experienced fishermen to the young men on merchant voyages is uncertain, but even a limited knowledge of navigation helped close the social distance between master and crew.

Finally, the existence of fraternal and paternal bonds between master and crew can be gleaned from the decided lack of legal disputes. Both the Essex County Quarterly Courts (1640-1720) and the Massachusetts Vice-Admiralty Courts (1719-1750) contain only scattered cases in which a Salem master or seaman took the other to court. Far more frequent were disputes between masters and shipowners or merchants. An examination of the Quarterly Courts revealed that for the entire 1640-1720 period there were only seven actions between Salem masters and seamen compared to seventy between Salem masters and merchants.[24] In none of the seven was there a charge of coercion or brutality. Moreover, in neither the Quarterly nor the Vice-Admiralty Courts was there a single case of a Salem seaman deserting from a local vessel.

Another powerful factor which attracted the town's young men to the sea were the opportunities for promotion. With every vessel carrying a master and mate, in a crew of six one-third of the mariners were officers. If the officers were recruited from Salem's maritime community, then over time fifty percent of the town's seamen had an

---

[23] An example of this type of share system can be found in the William Pickering Account Ledgers.

[24] There were more disputes between masters and seamen in the court records than the seventy-eight mentioned above, but these involved non-residents. Most common were wage disputes and desertion involving British seamen and masters on British vessels.

opportunity for promotion.[25] Indeed, almost all promotions were confined to Salem men; even those from other communities within Essex County had little chance, even if they previously had held a mate or master's position in another New England port.[26] Only four of twenty-five master mariners were non-residents when they appeared in the portledge bills. This increased further the likelihood of advancement for Salem seaman and made a career at sea more attractive. In reality, the possibility of promotion was somewhat less, especially to the rank of master. The careers of master mariners were, on average, longer than mariners in the forecastle. An examination of those masters who had begun their careers before 1720 reveal that although some retired or died early, the majority continued to sail into their mid-forties. Figure 1 below lists the ages as a percentage, in five year groupings, of 132 shipmasters who sailed on 393 voyages between 1640 and 1720.[27]

Nevertheless, a large number of Salem seamen achieved the position of master mariner. Evidence for this can be obtained by comparing the names of seamen who appeared on both the portledge bills and the Salem tax lists to the names of masters listed in the customs and notarial records and later portledge bills. It was found that twenty-nine percent of Salem resident mariners who appeared on the portledge bills as seamen also turned up as masters at a later date, while another nine percent surfaced as mates.[28]

There was a tradition of seafaring among many Salem families. Some, such as the Graftons, made the transition to seafaring in the 1640s, and their descendants continued into the nineteenth century. The

---

[25] If there were a crew of six and two were officers, then ideally when both officers retired or died, two of the remaining crew of four would fill the vacancies. Thus, each had a fifty percent chance for promotion.

[26] Of those seamen listed in the portledge bills from 1745 to 1760 who later became masters or mates, all but two (one master and one mate) came from Salem.

[27] The actual number of shipmasters occupying each five year bracket were as follows: <20, 4; 20-24, 45; 25-29, 85; 30-34, 75; 35-39, 66; 40-44, 60; 45-49, 32; 50-54, 15; 55-59, 5; 60-64, 5; >64, 1; for a total of 393.

[28] Of immense help were the published customs records of vessels entering and clearing Salem between 1750 and 1769. See Harriet Silvester Tapley (ed.), *Early Coastwise and Foreign Shipping of Salem: A Record of the Entrances and Clearances of the Port of Salem, 1750-1769* (Salem, 1934).

majority of Salem resident mariners who sailed before 1720 had sons, nephews, grandsons, or grand-nephews who appeared on the portledge bills a generation later. But these vessels were not only manned by old Salem families: throughout the colonial period many new names appeared as well. Some were new residents, others were the sons of fathers who had arrived in Salem as labourers or tradesmen, and many were the offspring of old Salem families who were the first of their line to venture to sea. There was therefore both a tradition of seafaring and a constant influx of new recruits from the labouring and artisan classes. The core of new recruits came from these two sources.

**Figure 1
Percentage of Shipmasters Occupying
Five-Year Age Brackets**

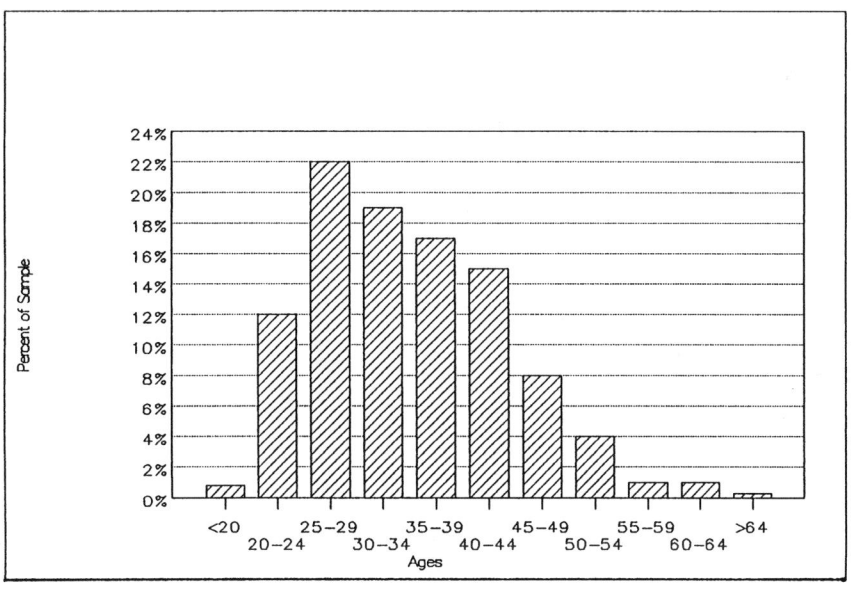

Source: George Francis Dow and Mary G. Thresher (eds.), *Records and Files of the Quarterly Courts of Essex County, Massachusetts* (9 vols., Salem, 1911-1975); Great Britain, Public Record Office. *Naval Officer Shipping Lists*, Colonial Office files, CO 5/749, CO 5/848, CO 27/12, CO 33/13-16, CO 41/6, CO 142/14, CO 157/1, CO 187/1-2, T 64/47; Essex Institute, *Vital Records of Salem, Massachusetts to 1849* (6 vols., Salem, 1916); Sidney Perley, *The History of Salem, Masachusetts* (3 vols., Salem, 1924).

Few masters were connected by blood or marriage to the vessel owners who hired them. The only connection was financial, for on occasion a master had shares in the vessel he commanded. The clearest proof of this is in the period 1697-1714, for which complete lists of shareholders for a number of Salem vessels have survived.[29] A comparison between the masters and shareholders of seventy vessels revealed only two blood connections and three relations by marriage. Sixty-five masters had no connection with the owners by blood or marriage; of these, seventeen had shares in the vessel.

From the beginning of the eighteenth century to the Revolution, Salem remained stable economically. An examination of wealth trends reveals this clearly. Salem was not Boston, and although there were a few families who may have approached the wealth of Boston's elite, most local merchants remained relatively poor cousins of the larger community to the south. Nor did the Salem master mariner achieve the wealth that his children or grandchildren would when they sailed to the East in the early nineteenth century. The cargoes carried by an eighteenth-century Salem vessel would have yielded minimal profits. Fish, timber, staves, wine, sugar, molasses and rum were typical and shipping them around the Atlantic in sloops and schooners was not the way to riches.

Salem's trading patterns remained stable up to the eve of the American Revolution, and so long as this continued so did its patterns of wealth. These patterns emerge when further examining the tax lists. Arranging the taxes for any one year into deciles, the ratio of wealth from one decile to the decile immediately lower was remarkably consistent from the beginning of the century to 1770.[30]

---

[29] As part of an effort by the Crown to ensure that trade within the Empire was carried in vessels owned solely by British investors, a 1696 act required the owners of any vessel trading with the colonies to swear an oath in writing describing the vessel, testifying to the place and date of its construction, listing its owners, and explicitly stating that no foreigner owned any shares. Also included were the name of the master and the vessel's type and tonnage. The records listing Massachusetts vessels have survived for the period 1697-1714. See Massachusetts Archives, "Massachusetts Vessel Registrations, 1697-1714."

[30] See Appendix A for a break down of these ratios. For the years 1683, 1690, and for each five year period following up to 1765, the taxes of every inhabitant within the town were listed and sorted according to value. Each list, i.e. each year, was then divided into deciles with the decile designated as first referring to those taxes belonging to the highest ten percent. The median value within each decile was used in calculating

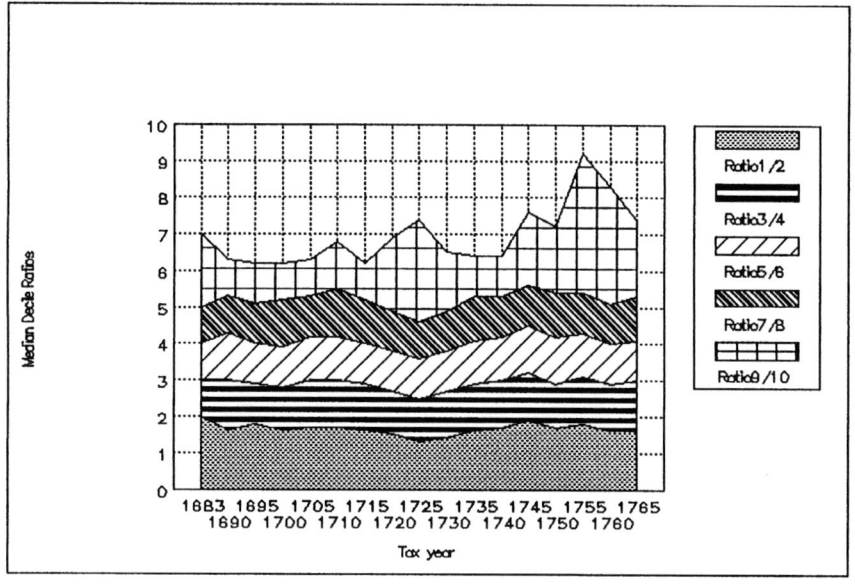

Figure 2
Selected Ratios of Median Decile Values

Source: Essex Institute, Salem Tax Lists, 1683, in *Essex County Quarterly Court Records*, IX, Salem Tax Lists, 1689-1776.

However, even adjusting for this limitation, this ratio must reflect a steadily worsening economic condition for this segment of Salem society. One large group making up this portion were people on fixed incomes such as widows receiving a stipend set by the probate courts. Gary Nash, in discussing the same period for Boston has argued that an economic gap between the top five percent and the remainder of Boston's society widened as the eighteenth century progressed. The most heavily affected groups, he argued, were mariners and widows who made up the majority of the population occupying the lowest thirty percent of Boston's economic hierarchy. According to Nash much of Boston's difficulties stemmed from the burden imposed upon the town from the several wars it had engaged in on behalf of Britain from 1689

---

the ratios. Appendix A listed the median value of decile and Appendix B listed the ratios between one median value and next one lower.

onward. Depreciation of the colony's currency, rising inflation, and the burden of public relief in the support of the many widows and children who had lost husbands during the conflict helped create the deteriorating conditions within Boston.[31]

Even if Salem was not spared this distress entirely, the stable ratios between one decile group and the next indicates that most of the town shared the burden proportionally. The only exception appears to have been the bottom five percent. This segment grew progressively poorer in relation to the rest of the town, particularly from 1745 onward. Nevertheless, because of the stability of wealth distribution in the top nine deciles, the social patriarchal structure of the town remained constant, and it is this stability which helps explain the stable recruitment patterns throughout the period.

Salem's shipping industry chose local mariners over outsiders for both social and economic reasons. The positive factors which attracted local men were reinforced by the town's dislike of strangers. This disquiet had its roots in the desire of the seventeenth-century Puritan to remain uncontaminated by outside influences and was often reflected in legislation. For example, Quakers were often denied permission to enter the colony. As early as 1650 masters or mates who brought strangers into the ports were required to present them before the governor, deputy governor or two magistrates, and outsiders were required to obtain permission to stay.[32] Puritans were very fearful about any stranger spiritually contaminating their community or becoming a charge on the public purse and did everything in their power to avoid it, including the hire of vessels to remove unwanted people from the colony.

Puritan charity did not extend to outsiders. A sad example of their insensitivity to strangers was found in the way residents of the Salem area treated an outsider in the winter of 1719. A mariner by the name of Thomas Crook came as a passenger from Ireland and landed somewhere in Maine. He arrived in Salem from Casco Bay sick and unfortunately penniless, but was turned away wherever he sought help. Eventually, he managed to trudge to Lynn, a community to the south,

---

[31]Gary B. Nash, *The Urban Crucible: Social Change, Political Consciousness, and the Origins of the American Revolution* (Cambridge, MA, 1979), 62-65.

[32]Nathaniel B. Shurtleff (ed.), *Records of the Governor and Company of the Massachusetts Bay in New England* (5 vols., Boston, 1853-1854), III, 205.

where he was unable to proceed any further because of his "perishing condition." The town, forced to put him under the care of the local doctor for six weeks, refused responsibility for the medical costs and petitioned the colony to reimburse the doctor. That Crook was not held responsible for the debt probably means he died from his illness.[33]

But shipowners and masters did not choose locals only because of a communal desire to avoid strangers. It appears to have been in the self-interest of all concerned to hire local men. Most Salem merchant vessels did not carry a supercargo and the numerous letters which merchants and shipowners gave to their masters in regard to the disposal of exports and the purchase of imports testify to the role the master played. Because merchants' marriage and blood relations did not often appear as masters, the former needed to rely on people whom they knew.[34] In turn, a master wanted a crew on whom he could rely. The uncertainty of a stranger was a factor he would prefer to avoid.

Was the maritime labour in Salem efficient in the sense that it resulted from free access between labour and management? Local men freely moved in and out of the labour market. The industry was able to recruit a sufficient supply of local labour because of strong positive inducements, the most important of which likely was the opportunity to achieve a higher economic and social status through promotion. But the market was closed to most outsiders. Vertical divisions existed because of the community's fear of aliens and because of self-interest. It has been well documented that workers in New England, including maritime labour, were more expensive than in Britain. With numerous desertions from British and foreign ships, Salem and all of New England easily could have tapped a ready supply of cheap labour. Yet in almost every case deserters, when caught, were returned to their vessels.[35] Salem

---

[33]This story came from the appendix of *The Acts and Resolves Public and Private of the Province of Massachusetts Bay*, IX, 658.

[34]The importance of the shipmaster's role as supercargo is further borne out when the court cases between merchant and shipmaster are further examined. The majority of cases involved a dispute over some aspect of freight. Few were related to the vessel itself.

[35]An examination of the Essex County Quarterly Court records, 1640-1720, and the Vice-Admiralty Court records, 1640-1750, shows that few deserters won their cases. In contrast, over ninety percent of mariners, whether locals or foreigners, won their cases

preferred to recruit more expensive local labour because of the generally amicable relations between master and crew. This harmony existed because of the paternal and fraternal bonds which defined shipboard relationships. The Salem maritime labour market was willing to pay a premium to obtain what it considered more reliable labour.

Within the confines of Salem a maritime labour market operated efficiently, but because outsiders were generally excluded, in relation to the rest of the maritime world it would have to be classed as inefficient. Still, because merchants were willing to pay a premium for labour, the extra cost must have been considered a good investment. If so, then it must be questioned whether free access to labour markets is a sufficient standard, at least in some circumstances, to judge labour market efficiency.

---

when they prosecuted their employers for wages. Almost without exception, mariners won wage disputes but lost when taken to court for desertion.

Appendix A
Median Value of Each Docile for Selected Tax Years

Tax Year	1	2	3	4	5	6	7	8	9	10
1683	96	48	36	36	24	24	24	24	24	12
1690	840	540	360	264	240	192	180	180	180	180
1695	180	102	72	64	54	48	42	37	27	24
1700	144	90	72	60	48	42	40	32	24	24
1705	1044	600	432	324	264	216	192	168	120	120
1710	936	552	396	300	240	204	180	144	120	96
1715	396	252	180	144	108	96	84	72	60	60
1720	269	177	136	109	96	86	82	75	68	34
1725	314	242	184	148	130	118	109	104	100	36
1730	142	101	81	63	54	49	45	41	39	25
1735	593	368	280	217	172	144	128	110	100	88
1740	507	301	229	170	133	109	93	85	78	73
1745	732	384	294	228	178	138	114	102	96	48
1750	1590	926	724	583	456	354	303	252	233	132
1755	547	312	232	172	128	110	100	92	76	20
1760	1188	736	528	404	337	297	264	231	191	60
1765	629	391	273	202	163	142	137	112	91	44

Sources: See figure 2.

Appendix B
Ratios of Median Decile Values for Selected Tax Years

Tax Year	1/2	2/3	3/4	4/5	5/6	6/7	7/8	8/9	9/10
1683	2.0	1.3	1.0	1.5	1.0	1.0	1.0	1.0	2.0
1690	1.6	1.5	1.4	1.1	1.3	1.1	1.0	1.0	1.0
1695	1.8	1.4	1.1	1.2	1.1	1.1	1.1	1.4	1.1
1700	1.6	1.3	1.2	1.3	1.2	1.1	1.3	1.3	1.0
1705	1.7	1.4	1.3	1.2	1.2	1.1	1.1	1.4	1.0
1710	1.7	1.4	1.3	1.3	1.2	1.1	1.3	1.2	1.3
1715	1.6	1.4	1.3	1.3	1.1	1.2	1.2	1.2	1.0
1720	1.5	1.3	1.2	1.1	1.1	1.0	1.1	1.1	1.0
1725	1.3	1.3	1.2	1.1	1.1	1.1	1.0	1.0	2.0
1730	1.4	1.2	1.3	1.2	1.1	1.1	1.1	1.1	2.8
1735	1.6	1.3	1.3	1.3	1.2	1.1	1.2	1.1	1.6
1740	1.7	1.3	1.3	1.3	1.2	1.2	1.1	1.1	1.1
1745	1.9	1.3	1.3	1.3	1.3	1.2	1.1	1.1	1.1
1750	1.7	1.3	1.2	1.3	1.3	1.2	1.2	1.1	2.0
1755	1.8	1.3	1.3	1.3	1.2	1.1	1.1	1.2	1.8
1760	1.6	1.4	1.3	1.2	1.1	1.1	1.1	1.2	3.8
1765	1.6	1.4	1.4	1.2	1.1	1.0	1.2	1.2	3.2
									2.1

Sources: See figure 2.

Mariners and Markets in the Age of Sail: The Case of the Netherlands

Paul C. van Royen

Introduction

In 1992 Charles P. Kindleberger, internationally esteemed as a distinguished professor of economics but less well known as a cadet, ordinary seaman and deckboy, published an interesting short volume on a subject that has recently become *en vogue*: maritime labour markets.[1] In *Mariners and Markets* Professor Kindleberger attempts to synthesize much of the research on various aspects of maritime labour that has appeared during the last couple of decades. Unfortunately, many of these publications leave the reader with more questions than answers.[2] In that sense it is understandable that someone might succumb to the urge — especially when for old time's sake his heart longs for the deep blue sea — to try to fit all the pieces of the maritime puzzle together to create a clear and consistent picture of the social side of seafaring. It is also conceivable that one might overlook the fact that it is at best debatable whether such a task is possible.[3]

---

[1]In October 1994 the Institute of Maritime History in The Hague organized a workshop on "The European Sailor, 1570-1870." The results will be published in *Research in Maritime History*, No. 10 (June 1996).

[2]See for instance P.C. van Royen, "Personnel of the Dutch and English Mercantile Marines (1700-1850). An Introductory Paper," in J.R. Bruijn and W.F.J. Mörzer Bruyns (eds.), *Anglo-Dutch Mercantile Marine Relations 1700-1850* (Amsterdam, 1991), especially 103-105.

[3]For the "larger" concepts see, for example, F. Braudel, *The Mediterranean and the Mediterranean World in the Age of Philip II* (2 vols., New York, 1973); and I. Wallerstein, *The Modern World-System II — Mercantilism and the Consolidation of the European World-Economy, 1600-1750* (New York, 1980).

It is obvious that Professor Kindleberger was intellectually stimulated – or irritated – to write his survey of maritime labour markets by statements about its efficiency. Some work on nineteenth-century New Bedford whaling, which claimed that markets were efficient – that is, that supply and demand were in harmony or at least moving towards a kind of equilibrium – apparently provided the impetus. Employee and employer, it was claimed, co-existed peacefully and were free to decline employment if wage levels were acceptable. Moreover, the market was "populated by rational, intelligent, informed and maximizing individuals who make decisions independently."[4]

There are good reasons to doubt the global validity of such statements. As Professor Kindleberger rightly notes, "crimping" and "shanghaiing" were common and neither implies freedom of choice. In short, there appears to be a gap between theory and reality. Moreover, it is doubtful whether the concept of efficiency – whatever it may mean – will help to deepen our understanding of how maritime labour markets functioned in the age of sail. Or to put it in the form of a question, is it plausible that a maritime labour market – independent of "national" labour markets – existed? In this paper I shall try to examine whether the notion of efficiency helps us to understand the Dutch maritime labour market better. For reasons to be explained later, I will concentrate on the first subjects tackled by Kindleberger: recruitment and pay.

The Dutch Labour Market, 1500-1800

In many respects the success of the Dutch economy was miraculous both to contemporaries and historians. After 1450 the economy and population base expanded rapidly and burst the constraints of Malthusian checks and balances.[5] Indeed, there was real economic growth, a phenomenon that made the Netherlands an exception in Western Europe, where there was hardly any real expansion. By the early sixteenth century both nominal and real wages in Holland were the highest in the region. This first era of economic growth lasted until the middle of the seventeenth century

---

[4]Charles P. Kindleberger, *Mariners and Markets* (London, 1992), xi-xii.

[5]Jan de Vries, "The Labour Market," *Economic and Social History in the Netherlands*, IV (1993), 55-78. The larger part of this survey also can be found in J.R. Bruijn and J. Lucassen (eds.), *Op de schepen der Oost-Indische Compagnie. Vijf artikelen van J. de Hullu* (Groningen, 1980), 11-29.

and in general was characterized by a substantial demand for labour, an enormous demographic increase (between 1570 and 1620 the population nearly doubled), rapidly rising nominal wages, small price increases, and growing real wages. The proportion of the populace living in cities rose to sixty percent. Immigration and the Reformation also led to an increase in the size of the labour force. It was only at the end of this expansionary era that prices began to outstrip wages.

In the century after 1650 population and nominal wages both stagnated. Due to slowly falling prices real wages rose, but a new spectre – unemployment – reared its head. Whether the Dutch economy reached a kind of balance or declined is still a matter of debate. Nonetheless, it is clear that while some branches of economic activity did show signs of decline, others remained level or even increased.

After 1750 nominal wages stagnated, population increased, prices rose and real wages fell. Due to a virtual absence of new economic opportunities, structural unemployment became entrenched. Yet as Jaap Bruijn and Jan Lucassen have warned, in the Netherlands it is prudent to treat macro-level variables like wages, prices, employment and population with care, since regional differences were often extreme.[6] Still, as Jan de Vries has argued, "by the third quarter of the seventeenth century the fluid labour market that characterized the preceding era of rapid economic growth was assuming the shape it would have for the next century and more."[7] The Dutch labour market of the sixteenth and seventeenth centuries was dynamic, but in the eighteenth it reflected a kind of social "segmentation," consisting of relatively secure "core" work, casual labour, and jobs of last resort. Before asking if the market was efficient, let us look at the Dutch maritime labour market.

The Dutch Maritime Labour Market

For the development of the maritime labour market we have to rely almost completely on Bruijn's and Lucassen's research.[8] Actually, little is known about it, especially in relation to the overall labour market.

---

[6]Bruijn and Lucassen (eds.), *Op de schepen*, 12.

[7]De Vries, "The Labour Market," 68.

[8]Bruijn and Lucassen (eds.), *Op de schepen*, 26-29.

Although some important historical demographic research has been done, especially by members of the "Wageningen school," no consistent picture has yet emerged of the overall development of the Dutch labour market.[9] Neither de Vries' article nor the contents of a special issue of the *Tijdschrift voor Sociale Geschiedenis* could fill this vacuum.[10]

As for the maritime labour market, the picture we have seems relatively accurate.[11] The demand for maritime labour was most impressive during the first half of the seventeenth century. During that time, the merchant marine conquered all European waters from the White Sea to the Mediterranean, while the Dutch East India Company (*Verenigde Oostindische Compagnie*, or VOC) and, a bit later, the West India Company (*Westindische Compagnie*) and the whaling industry hoisted their sails as well. In addition, a well-equipped navy had to protect the merchant marine. This means that about 1610, 33,000 sailors were needed to man all these ships – merchantmen, VOC and naval. By 1680 employment had risen to 50,000, while at the end of the eighteenth century nearly 45,000 sailors still earned their daily bread at sea. Yet these crude numbers do not provide much insight into the intriguing and complex world of recruitment and employment because a general approach does no justice to the various groups operating in this market. One should distinguish between the companies and the navy, the merchant marine and whaling, and finally coastal and deep-sea fisheries. It is only through such distinctions that we can analyse the various patterns of recruitment, origins, wages, and the like. This suggests that a strategy of treating maritime labour markets as homogeneous is likely to be unproductive.

---

[9]B.H. Slicher van Bath, *Een samenleving onder spanning. Geschiedenis van het platteland in Overijssel* (Assen, 1957); J.A. Faber, *Drie eeuwen Friesland. Economische en sociale ontwikkelingen van 1500 tot 1800* (Wageningen, 1972); A.M. van der Woude, *Het Noorderkwartier. Een regionaal historisch onderzoek in de demografische en economische geschiedenis van westelijk Nederland van de late Middeleeuwen tot het begin van de negentiende eeuw* (Wageningen, 1972).

[10]De Vries, "The Labour Market." The special issue of *Tijdschrift voor Sociale Geschiedenis* was XIII (November 1987).

[11]For employment of the various branches of shipping through the ages, see van Royen, "Personnel," 107; P.C. van Royen, "Manning the Merchant Marine: The Dutch Maritime Labour Market about 1700," *International Journal of Maritime History*, I, No. 1 (June 1989), 1-28.

For this reason I have chosen to exclude whaling and fishing from the following analysis. Whaling has been studied extensively by L. Hacquebord and P. Dekker.[12] While the sources for coastal and deep-sea fisheries are scanty, some important recent research has been completed by A.P. van Vliet.[13] The fact that fishing was limited to a handful of villages along the west and southwest coast of Holland and Enkhuizen more or less confirms the limitations of any global concept like efficiency.

On the manning of the VOC we know quite a bit. Because of the research of Jaap Bruijn and his students at the University of Leiden we are well informed about the total numbers of seamen and their origins over two centuries.[14] From the very beginning employment with the VOC grew rapidly, from 2000 seamen in 1610 to 8500 in 1680, before slowing to stand at only 11,500 in 1770. Over time the origins of VOC seamen also changed. In the sixteenth century about seventy-five percent originated from the coastal provinces of the Dutch Republic, in particular the province of Holland (ninety percent), and especially from the cities (ninety percent of Holland's total). Thus, VOC sailors were recruited mainly from Holland's cities. About twenty-five percent of the sailors were foreigners, most originating from maritime districts in Scandinavia and Germany.

During the eighteenth century, by which time demographic growth had virtually ended and the Dutch economy was relatively stagnant, the share of foreign seamen started to rise rapidly, reaching

---

[12]An up-to-date survey of research on the history of whaling can be found in Louwrens Hacquebord, "Van Noordse Compagnie tot Maatschappij voor de Walvisvaart. Honderd jaar onderzoek naar de geschiedenis van de Nederlandse walvisvaart," *Tijdschrift voor Zeegeschiedenis*, XIII (May 1994), 19-40.

[13]A.P. van Vliet, *Vissers en Kapers. De zeevisserij vanuit het Maasmondgebied en de Duinkerker kapers (ca. 1580-1648)* ('s-Gravenhage, 1994), 40-41.

[14]J.R. Bruijn, "De personeelsbehoefte van de VOC overzee en aan boord, bezien in Aziatisch en Nederlands perspectief," *Bijdragen en Mededelingen betreffende de Geschiedenis der Nederlanden*, XCI (1976), 218-248. See also Bruijn and Lucassen (eds.), *Op de schepen*, 134-140. Detailed studies of Delft are K.L. Schouwenburg, "Het personeel op de schepen van de Kamer Delft der VOC in de eerste helft der 18e eeuw," *Tijdschrift voor Zeegeschiedenis*, VII (May 1988), 76-93; and Schouwenburg, "Het personeel op de schepen van de Kamer Delft der VOC in de tweede helft der 18e eeuw," *Tijdschrift voor Zeegeschiedenis*, VIII (October 1989), 179-186.

more than fifty percent by 1800. Moreover, the number of "sailors" originating from inland regions of Europe grew substantially. The VOC was clearly the principal source of this demand. At the beginning of the seventeenth century only six percent of seamen served in the VOC, while by 1800 more than twenty-five percent did. This growing share, however, cannot be explained by higher wages, since these had been static since 1636.

Information on the sailors aboard Dutch men-of-war is more sparse. In *The Dutch Navy of the Seventeenth and Eighteenth Centuries*, Jaap Bruijn provides a fairly sophisticated map to manning developments in the various chapter and sub-chapter titles: "truly international crews," "well-manned ships," and "naval seaman, a poor man's job."[15] Indeed, available evidence indicates that by the beginning of the seventeenth century many foreigners enlisted in the Dutch navy, while in the second half of the century more Dutchmen tried their luck.[16] By the time the Dutch Republic became a secondary power, a growing share of foreigners again populated the lower decks. While in the seventeenth century it was no problem to find men to man the fleet for yet another war with England or France, it became increasingly difficult to recruit sailors in the eighteenth. Like their counterparts in the VOC, those in the navy increasingly came from urban areas.[17]

---

[15]Jaap R. Bruijn, *The Dutch Navy of the Seventeenth and Eighteenth Centuries* (Columbia, SC, 1993).

[16]According to Bruijn, *The Dutch Navy*, 55, 133, 139, the relative geographical origins of crew on Zeeland men-of-war were as follows:

	ca. 1600	1669	1694	1709	ca. 1770
Flushing	21	42	7	18	1
Zeeland	13	18	10	19	5
Holland	10	8	36	14	29
Netherlands	7	7	10	4	7
Foreign	46	22	35	44	57
Unknown	3	3	2	1	1

[17]See also C.R. Boxer, "Sedentary Workers and Seafaring Folk in the Dutch Republic," in J.S. Bromley and E.H. Kossman (eds.), *Britain and the Netherlands* (2 vols., Groningen, 1964), II, 148-168; Bruijn and Lucassen (eds.), *Op de schepen*, 19.

As far as these two "segments" of the maritime labour market are concerned, it is evident that the various developments had everything to do with larger political, economic and social trends within the Dutch Republic. The same can be said for the merchant marine, although this branch of maritime activities was populated by a different kind of seaman, recruited from a different social and economic echelon.[18] At the beginning of the seventeenth century, merchant mariners accounted for more than sixty percent (21,500) of total seaborne employment in the various Dutch fleets. In the eighteenth century this share declined to about forty-five percent, although the absolute decline (to 21,000) was less stark. There are some indications that before the mid-seventeenth century some fluidity of employment might have existed between the various branches of shipping.[19] Thereafter, switching from one branch to another was exceptional. While in some respects the VOC and naval labour markets were similar to that in which merchant seamen were recruited, a closer look shows some important differences. For instance, unlike the VOC and the navy the merchant marine was populated mainly by seamen from the rural areas of Holland, Friesland and the Wadden Islands (in the north of the Netherlands). While on board VOC and naval ships hardly any regional or family ties can be discerned, the merchant marine exhibited a strong geographic relationship.[20] In the course of the eighteenth century this cohesion slowly withered, only to be restored after the Napoleonic wars.[21] But by that time the geographic origins of Dutch sailors had completely altered.

While foreigners were quite common among merchant crews, they never outnumbered the native-born. By the end of the seventeenth century about twenty-five percent of merchant seamen originated from abroad. Seventy years later this share had increased to more than fifty percent. Within this foreign share there were also some changes in place of origin. While Scandinavians had previously comprised the majority of

---

[18]P.C. van Royen, *Zeevarenden op de koopvaardijvloot omstreeks 1700* (Amsterdam, 1987).

[19]Bruijn, *The Dutch Navy*, 40-53.

[20]The details are in van Royen, *Zeevarenden* and "Manning the Merchant Marine."

[21]Van Royen, "Personnel," 108-112.

foreigners, in the second half of the century they were replaced by sailors from northern Germany.[22]

In general, the various changes in recruitment by the VOC, navy and merchant marine reflected broader developments in the Netherlands, especially during the eighteenth century. This observation reinforces the danger of trying to separate maritime labour from the larger domestic labour pool.

Table 1
Monthly Wages of VOC, Navy and Merchant Marine,
1700-1826 (guilders)

	VOC 17th-18th cent.	Navy	Merchant Marine			
			1700/10	1774/75	1814/16	1824/26
Master	60-80	30	-	-	-	-
First Mate	40-50	36	32	31.60	32	32
Bosun	20	22	-	23.40	29	28
Carpenter	30-36	28	32	31.70	31	25
Cook	20	18	25	19.80	22	21
AB	7-11	11	10-15	14.50	22	20
OS	6-7	-	-	-	17	14
Boy	4-6	4-7	5-8	-	9	8

Sources: J. Lucassen, "Zeevarenden," *Maritieme Geschiedenis der Nederlanden*, II (1977), 141; Jaap R. Bruijn, *The Dutch Navy of the Seventeenth and Eighteenth Centuries* (Columbia, SC, 1993), 199; G.K. Pielage and M.J. Ramler, "Wie monsterden aan in 1774 en 1775. Een onderzoek naar de Nederlandse vrachtvaart en haar bemanning" (Unpublished paper, Free University of Amsterdam, 1990), tables 10-18; Municipal Archives, Amsterdam (MAA), Rechterlijk Archief PA 5061, 2618; MAA, Archief Waterschout PA 38, 91-94, 126-127.

Wages

If efficiency were of major importance in the Dutch maritime labour market, the effects should be easy to discern. In particular, wages in the various branches of shipping and regions of recruitment should be at

---

[22]The same kind of pattern can be observed with the crews of whaling vessels. This branch of maritime activity was concentrated in the northern part of Holland and on the Wadden Islands.

least broadly similar. Indeed, the wages presented in table 1 seem to reflect a rather stable reality. Before analysing them, it should be stressed that the various data should be interpreted with care. As far as the remuneration paid by the VOC and the navy were concerned, nominal levels remained stagnant for nearly 200 years. The wages of 1700-1710 paid by the merchant marine should only be used as indicators. For instance, the cook's wages (twenty-five guilders a month) are not necessarily representative. The wages of the first mate, bosun, carpenter and cook seem to remain rather stable during the eighteenth century. Yet these ranks were paid at least the same or better by the VOC and the navy. Concerning the "lower" ranks — and they comprised the majority on East Indiamen — ABs and boys were better off in the merchant marine, particularly taking into account that sailing in European waters was healthier than travelling to the East Indies.

The changes in the various wages that can be observed after the Napoleonic wars were mainly caused by structural changes in the manning system. While before 1800 nearly every Dutch ship carried a bosun, this rank more or less disappeared in the nineteenth century, especially aboard smaller vessels. This also applies to the carpenter, who was replaced by a *klamphouder*, really an AB who was paid slightly more. In the case of ABs and OSs, the decrease in their wages was mainly a result of the intake of younger, less experienced sailors. The differences between the wages of 1700-1710 and those at the beginning of the nineteenth century can be partially explained by the fact that in the earlier period maritime labour was easy to recruit in the Dutch Republic (especially Holland), while a century later it was harder to get the right men to fill the "lower" ranks.

Moreover, nation-wide merchant wages hide some significant regional differences (see table 2). It is amazing how Frisian mates, boatswains, and cooks were underpaid relative to their colleagues from Amsterdam, North Holland, the Wadden Islands and even from abroad. At the ranks of mate and carpenter, foreigners also earned less than native-borne recruits; indeed, the mates originating from the Wadden Islands were paid best while Amsterdam carpenters topped this rank. Research in a later period (1834-1836) by and large confirms these findings.[23]

---

[23]A. Verburg, "Zeelieden aan boord van Nederlandse vrachtschepen 1834-1836" (Unpublished paper, University of Amsterdam, 1990), table 7.

Table 2
Monthly Wages of Merchant Marine,
per rank and region, 1774-1775 (guilders)

	1 mate	bosun	carpenter	cook	seaman
Amsterdam	33.80	23.20	33.40	20.30	14.10
North Holland	34.00	23.70	32.80	20.70	14.20
Friesland	23.50	22.10	30.10	18.40	14.70
Wadden Is.	35.80	23.60	32.60	21.60	14.00
Foreigners	30.30	23.40	30.00	20.10	14.20

Source: Pielage and Ramler, "Wie monsterden," tables 10-23.

Conclusion

Instability and the vicissitudes of life characterized the rise and fall of an economy in pre-industrial society. The network of relations in pre-industrial economies was relatively incoherent due to technical and institutional imperfections.[24] General trends and developments are in the eye of the beholder, although they need not be.

Before we get to the heart of the matter of efficiency in maritime labour markets, it might be helpful to remember some lines by Peter Musgrave about "the economics of uncertainty." The prevailing optimism, with its obsession with growth and its roots may have been justifiable in modern economic history; for the pre-modern and medieval worlds, it has involved a distortion not merely of the facts but also of attitudes. Recent work in the history of this period has clearly shown the importance of "destabilizing" factors, events and situations which, for long periods could halt or reverse the "process of growth." There is, indeed, a more fundamental objection to the transference of "growth economics" to a world in which the expectation of continued growth did not exist. The study of *mentalités* suggests that men in the past had very different attitudes toward the economy. These opinions created an approach to economic life dominated by general uncertainty rather than

---

[24]P.W. Klein, "De zeventiende eeuw 1585-1700," in J.H. van Stuijvenberg (ed.), *De economische geschiedenis van Nederland* (Groningen, 1979), 79-118.

by some expectation based on long-term growth.[25] There is no doubt that Musgrave (and many others) are right. Uncertainty ruled the economy. A "transparent" economy, with free flows of information and a unified labour market with open access, was nonexistent in pre-industrial society.

The only conclusions we can draw are that there is no clear evidence in the Netherlands of an efficient labour market. Instead, we can see enormous differences in wages (and prices) and a kind of segmentation, described by Jan de Vries, into at least three distinct maritime labour markets – and this, remember, excludes whaling and fishing. This suggests that efficiency had little to do with the way the Dutch maritime labour market was organized.

Even our rational *homo economicus* sometimes is hard to find. Although German migrants knew that it could be hell to sail with the VOC, they still came and joined, many never to return. During the seventeenth century the Dutch navy had no serious problems manning ships, but in the eighteenth, when the Dutch engaged in hardly any wars, it became increasingly difficult to find qualified sailors. Obviously, the rationale for deciding whether to join the navy must have been different.

This is the heart of the matter. Those who used the concept of efficiency to explain productivity in nineteenth-century New Bedford whaling are not to be blamed. They stuck to their trade, whaling, in nineteenth-century Massachusetts. Professor Kindleberger, however, seems to have forgotten the limits not only of the subject but also of time, place, and space. His attempt to create a clear picture of the subject has failed miserably. There is nothing wrong with the concept of efficiency, but it is quite evident that it cannot be used – and so far has not been used – as a means to understand the way maritime labour markets functioned. On the contrary, it blurs the picture, as Professor Kindleberger should have noticed when he started to write his book.[26] In my opinion, it would have been better if he had applied his prodigious talents to a different subject.

---

[25]P. Musgrave, "The Economics of Uncertainty: The Structural Revolution in the Spice Trade, 1480-1640," in P.L. Cottrell and D.H. Aldcroft (eds.), *Shipping, Trade and Commerce. Essays in Memory of Ralph Davis* (Leicester, 1981), especially 10.

[26]Kindleberger, *Mariners and Markets*, xvii.

Pirates and Markets

David J. Starkey

Attacks upon seaborne trade were a persistent and important feature of the Atlantic empires established by European maritime powers in the early modern era. Such assaults were often perpetrated by the crews of naval and privateering vessels sanctioned by their respective states to commit acts of violence upon specified targets – usually enemy traders in wartime. At the same time, this colonial and commercial world attracted and spawned a range of predators whose operations were deemed illegal by contemporaries. Such commerce-raiders were viewed as pirates. Of course, this was a highly subjective viewpoint, for the law of the sea was more a reflection of the prevailing balance of state power than an impartial interpretation of natural justice.[1] In reality, the pirates included not only stereotypical, stateless sea-robbers, but also such predators as the Barbary corsairs and Caribbean buccaneers, whose actions were licensed by authorities largely beyond the control of the metropolitan seats of imperial power. This paper is concerned with the various forms of piracy which fell within this imprecise parameter.

At the heart of the discussion is the contention that piracy, for all its political and social ramifications, was essentially an economic activity; that men, and occasionally women, attacked and plundered shipping to generate income for themselves.[2] Though its extent and impact fluctuated greatly, piracy at certain times and in particular regions assumed the

---

[1] Anne Pérotin-Dumon, "The Pirate and the Emperor: Power and the Law on the Seas, 1450-1850," in James D. Tracy (ed.), *The Political Economy of Merchant Empires* (New York, 1991), 196-227.

[2] See John L. Anderson, "Piracy in the Eastern Seas, 1750-1850: Some Economic Implications," in J.A. de Moor and E. van Eyck van Heslinga (eds.), *Pirates and Privateers: New Perspectives on Piracy and Privateering in the 18th and 19th Centuries* (Exeter, forthcoming).

proportions of a large-scale business, significant enough to attract the repressive attentions of maritime states. Often located physically and socially on the margins of the Atlantic economy, this business was inextricably linked to its market mechanisms. In providing goods and services to a range of consumers by deploying a variety of resources, piracy was a facet of the markets which governed trading and shipping activity. At the same time, it was largely a function of these markets, for it tended to emerge and thrive at the junctures when disequilibria were evident between demand and supply. The extent to which such market inefficiencies precipitated piratical activity is the main concern of this paper. To this end, attention is focused on three aspects of the subject. First, the principal forms of Atlantic piracy in the early modern era are identified; then, the market forces which conditioned the pirate's business are analysed; and finally, the causes and incidence of piratical activity are related to the wider question of the efficiency of the market for seafarers in the age of sail.[3]

Waves of Piracy

Piracy is a service industry, a business concerned with the transport and distribution, rather than the production, of commodities. Seaborne trade is a prerequisite of this activity, although as in any form of predatory enterprise the very success of the hunter necessarily affects the extent of the prey. Market forces condition the scale, incidence and character of this business. On the demand side, pirates consume the goods they steal, or else deliver them to buyers who are rarely the intended recipients but consumers in alternative markets.[4] Moreover, while the interests of states might be served by piratical activity, for this consumer the service provided is usually military rather than commercial. On the supply side, piracy is sustained by three principal production factors – land (ports and bases), labour (seafarers), and capital (vessels, provisions, arms, etc.). Yet instead of competing in factor markets, the pirate obtains resources by stealing or else by deploying idle vessels, equipment and labour. Intervening substantially in this market, of course, is the state. While

---

[3]Charles P. Kindleberger, *Mariners and Markets* (London, 1992), 83.

[4]In this respect, piracy may be viewed as a form of social banditry. See E.J. Hobsbawm, *Bandits* (London, 1969), 71-79.

piracy by definition is illegal, variable factors like political will, commercial interest and naval capability greatly influence the colour and effectiveness of a government's interventionist policies.

This market structure strongly resembles the shipping industry. Shippers, like pirates, depend on the existence of seaborne trade, as well as serving the needs of consumers and states and drawing upon supplies of land, capital and labour. But there are critical differences between the two. The role of government differs, for states generally seek to encourage their shipping industries; protection against pirates was one measure customarily adopted to meet this end. A further contrast lies in the relationships between shipping and piracy on the one hand, and trade on the other. Shipping relates to trade symbiotically, an increase or decrease in one normally leading to gains or losses in the other. Piracy, by contrast, is parasitic, feeding not only on the goods transported but also on the resources deployed by the carrier. The markets which shippers serve, and in which they engage, are therefore highly significant to the level of piratical as well as shipping activity. But piracy is not a simple parasite, expanding or contracting in line with its host.[5] Rather, as a rival with – and predator upon – the interests of traders and shippers, piracy tends to exploit market deficiencies, flourishing at times when substantial disequilibria emerge between the demand and supply of commodities, military services and the production factors of shippers.

Activity rates reflect the contrasts between shipping and piracy. Whereas the former is a more or less constant, albeit fluctuating, form of enterprise, piracy is largely a product of particular, often short-term, conditions. It is therefore volatile, a contention borne out by the pattern of piratical activity evident in the Atlantic between the early seventeenth century and the 1830s. Of course, measuring the scale of piracy with any precision is difficult due to the fragmentary nature of the surviving evidence. Nevertheless, sufficient data exist to offer an outline of the course of the business of piracy in the Atlantic economy of the early modern era. Though countless, incidental, petty acts of maritime lawlessness doubtless occurred, piracy as a large-scale business activity proceeded in five waves of varying duration and amplitude. Originating in, and impacting upon, different regions and facets of this trading system, each of the waves constituted a problem, and sometimes an opportunity, for the European maritime states.

---

[5]Anderson, "Piracy in the Eastern Seas."

Two of these piratical phenomena – Barbary piracy and Caribbean buccaneering – might be described as "long" waves, in that both were relatively durable maritime activities. While the so-called Barbary pirates were active more or less continuously in the Mediterranean, and occasionally in the eastern Atlantic, from the Middle Ages to the nineteenth century, buccaneering emerged in the early seventeenth century and remained a factor in the Caribbean until at least the 1690s.[6] There were other similarities between these two commerce-raiding genres. In the strictest sense, neither was piratical. The corsairs of North Africa cruised against Christian shipping with the spiritual blessing of Mohammed and the temporal authority of the Sultan, although they were generally regarded as pirates by European statesmen who likened their activities to a thorn in the foot, a painful irritant requiring a remedy.[7] Likewise, many of the great buccaneering forays against the Spanish Main were afforded a veneer of legitimacy by letters of marque issued by colonial authorities, even though the aims and means of these operations were clearly piratical.[8] Significantly, despite their dubious legality, both the Barbary corsairs and the Caribbean buccaneers served the interests of states, though not always overtly and sometimes inadvertently, by preying upon the commerce of political and commercial rivals.

In other respects, these long waves of piracy differed greatly. Essentially, the Barbary corsairs were the naval arm of Islam engaged in Eternal War with Christendom. Their operations therefore threatened the commerce and shipping of the principal European maritime states, though the nature and extent of the menace varied. In the early seventeenth century, the trading interests of England, Holland and Spain were damaged extensively by commerce-raiders based in Algiers, Sallee, Tunis and other North African ports. Abandoning oared galleys for sailing vessels, the Barbary corsairs ventured from their customary Mediterranean grounds to prey on the shipping lanes of the eastern Atlantic. While Spanish coastal and short-sea trade suffered great losses, it was the

---

[6]See Peter Earle, *Corsairs of Malta and Barbary* (London, 1970).

[7]David Delison Hebb, *Piracy and the English Government, 1616-1642* (Aldershot, 1994), 3.

[8]See Robert C. Ritchie, *Captain Kidd and the War against the Pirates* (Cambridge, MA, 1986).

English who were most vexed by their depredations, not least because they raided the coasts of southwestern England. With a "staggering" total of approximately 400 vessels and above 8000 captives carried to Barbary between 1616 and 1642, the English government was stirred to mount two naval campaigns and a series of diplomatic offensives to free hostages and reduce the "pirate scourge."[9] While these efforts had mixed results, the "Turkish menace" gradually receded from the 1640s by dint of treaties, tribute and threats of naval reprisal. Thereafter, the Barbary corsairs rarely passed the Straits – though as late as 1710 English East Indiamen were instructed to sail to the Orient "not in the way of the Algerine cruisers" -- and focused their aggression instead on the Christian privateers of Malta.[10] Though the scale of this activity diminished greatly in the eighteenth century, the coffers of the Barbary regencies nevertheless continued to be replenished by "safe passages" procured by Britain, France and other maritime powers.[11]

Buccaneering rendered military rather than financial services to the state. The origins of this somewhat nebulous breed of piracy can be traced to the outcasts, outlaws and interlopers who gained footholds in the Caribbean islands on the fringes of Spain's American Empire during the late sixteenth and early seventeenth centuries.[12] Surviving by hunting wild cattle, their number swelled in the 1630s and 1640s by those forced off the land by the advance of the plantation system, and by political refugees from Europe, these *boucaniers* gradually widened their predatory horizons to include Spanish vessels and goods passing close to

---

[9]Hebb, *Piracy*, 139-140.

[10]Great Britain, Public Record Office (PRO), High Court of Admiralty Papers (HCA) 26/14, Letter of Marque Declaration of Edmund Godfrey, Captain of the *Katherine*, 6 April 1710.

[11]Earle, *Corsairs of Malta and Barbary*, 36-46.

[12]Some interesting case studies are provided by David F. Marley, *Pirates and Engineers: Dutch and Flemish Adventurers in New Spain (1607-1697)* (Windsor, ON, 1992). For more general accounts, see A.H. Cooper-Prichard, *The Buccaneers: A Brief History* (Paris, 1927); Neil Grant, *Buccaneers* (London, 1976).

their bases.¹³ From such roots sprang the buccaneers of yore, who formed a potent, if irregular, military force in the Caribbean during the second half of the seventeenth century. Disowned in London, Paris and Amsterdam, yet commissioned concurrently in the West Indies, the buccaneers in effect were one of the main weapons with which Britain, France and the United Provinces sought to breach Spain's New World monopoly. Amid this war of attrition, the sack of Panama in 1670 by a division of buccaneers under Henry Morgan, the incursion of Bartholomew Sharp and over 1000 men into the Pacific in 1680-1681, and the attack on Veracruz by thirteen ships and 1400 buccaneers point to the scale and wider significance of this activity during an era in which there really was "no peace beyond the line."¹⁴ But towards the end of the seventeenth century, the conditions in which buccaneering developed and functioned passed, a change signalled by the French assault on Cartegena in 1697, in which "two societies, two conceptions of justice, collaborated and collided" in the combined force of regular troops from France and a company of unruly and increasingly anachronistic buccaneers.¹⁵

Such long waves of piratical activity were inextricably linked to the political and economic aspirations of the states, colonies or communities from which they emanated. Somewhat different in origin and effect were the comparatively brief surges of maritime lawlessness which occurred in the Atlantic between 1603 and 1616, 1714 and 1726, and 1815 and 1835. Similar patterns and characteristics can be perceived in these "short" waves of piracy. For instance, each followed a prolonged, wide-ranging war. Thus, the cessation of the Anglo-Spanish conflict of 1585-1603 heralded a burst of piratical aggression which originated in England but quickly spread to bases in southern Ireland and North

---

¹³Carl and Roberta Bridenbaugh, *No Peace Beyond the Line: The English in the Caribbean, 1624-1690* (New York, 1972), 175-176; Christopher Hill, "Radical Pirates?" in *The Collected Essays of Christopher Hill. Volume 3: People and Ideas in Seventeenth Century England* (Brighton, 1986), 161-187.

¹⁴Alexander O. Exquemelin, *The Buccaneers of America* (Amsterdam, 1678; reprint, Annapolis, 1993); Derek Howse and Norman J.W. Thrower (eds.), *A Buccaneer's Atlas: Basil Ringrose's South Sea Waggoner* (Berkeley, 1992); David F. Marley, *Sack of Veracruz: The Great Pirate Raid of 1683* (Windsor, ON, 1993).

¹⁵J.S. Bromley, "Outlaws at Sea, 1660-1720: Liberty, Equality and Fraternity among the Caribbean Freebooters," in J.S. Bromley (ed.), *Corsairs and Navies, 1660-1760* (London, 1987), 1.

Africa. Active in British coastal waters, the Western Approaches, off the Iberian peninsula and as far west as Newfoundland, these Jacobean pirates represented a serious threat to European traders and shippers, as well as a considerable diplomatic embarrassment to James I, the self-righteous, pirate-hating king of a "nation of pirates." At its height in 1608-1614, as many as 300 ships and 1000 men were engaged in piratical activity under the command of "admirals" such as Bishop, Jennings, Peter Easton and Henry Mainwaring. By 1615, however, this wave of piracy had lost momentum and within a year, much to James I's relief, the pirate menace had almost completely vanished.[16]

A century later, a similar cycle of lawlessness followed the peace of Utrecht. Though the epicentre of this eruption was the Caribbean, its tremors were felt in the Bahamas, the Carolinas and as far away as West Africa and the Indian Ocean. It has been estimated that up to 5000 freebooters were active at some stage during this wave of North American piracy in which such legendary characters as Edward Teach ("Blackbeard"), William Sawkins, Stede Bonnet and Bartholomew Roberts played prominent roles.[17] Related in a number of respects to the buccaneering of the previous generation, this wave of piracy was marked by an anarchic, anti-authoritarian strain which has become the stuff of legends. It was a passing phase, however, lasting for a decade or so, before abating amid much violence in the mid-1720s.[18]

In the early nineteenth century, a further piratical wave developed in the Caribbean. This *course independante*, like buccaneering and Barbary commerce-raiding, had pretensions of legitimacy in that it was integral to the wars of liberation which convulsed Spain's American Empire during and after the Napoleonic wars. As such, much piratical activity was undertaken by predators armed with commissions granted by revolutionary regimes, most notably the Carthaganian Republic and the

---

[16] Clive M. Senior, *A Nation of Pirates: English Piracy in its Heyday* (Newton Abbot, 1976); Hebb, *Piracy*, 7-11.

[17] See Philip Gosse, *The History of Piracy* (London, 1932), 176-212.

[18] Ritchie, *Captain Kidd*, 1-26; Marcus Rediker, *Between the Devil and the Deep Blue Sea: Merchant Seamen, Pirates and the Anglo-American Maritime World, 1700-1750* (Cambridge, 1987), 254-287.

Confederation of South American States.[19] Yet it was more akin to the lawless surges of 1603-1616 and 1714-1726. While it was closely linked to the onset of peace, it was also relatively short-lived and spatially dynamic, the focus of operations shifting from the West Indies to Columbia, Mexico, Buenos Aires and thence to Cuba, around whose shores fishermen-pirates continued to operate to great effect into the 1830s. As in the earlier short waves, pirate operations were on a large scale and, significantly, did not serve but threatened the commercial interests of European maritime states. The business of piracy, in each case, was therefore deemed beyond the law and confronted by naval forces dispatched to eradicate, reduce or at least police it. In the early seventeenth century, Dutch warships cruised against pirates based in southern Ireland while a Spanish fleet destroyed the pirate stronghold of Mamora in North Africa in July 1614.[20] Likewise, the British navy, supported by the bureaucracy and courts of the Admiralty, was charged with eliminating North American piracy in the 1710s and 1720s.[21] A century later it performed more of a restraining role, diverting the energies of the *course independante* away from British interests in the western hemisphere.[22]

A further common trait lay in the composition and structure of pirate crews and communities. The short waves of piracy – and buccaneering – were marked by the cosmopolitan character of the personnel involved and the egalitarian, democratic values which permeated their

---

[19]See Anne Pérotin-Dumon, "La contribution des *corsarios insurgentes* à l'independance americaine: course et piraterie dans le golfe du Mexique et la mer des Antilles, 1810-1830," in Michel Mollat (ed.), *Course et piraterie* (2 vols., Paris, 1975), II, 666-675; Basil Lubbock, *Cruisers, Corsairs and Slavers: An Account of the Suppression of the Picaroon, Pirate and Slaver by the Royal Navy during the 19th Century* (Glasgow, 1993), 59-72.

[20]Clive M. Senior, "The Confederation of Deep-Sea Pirates: English Pirates in the Atlantic 1603-25," in Mollat (ed.), *Course et piraterie*, I, 347-348.

[21]Rediker, *Between the Devil and the Deep Blue Sea*, 254-287; Carl E. Swanson, *Predators and Prizes: American Privateering and Imperial Warfare, 1739-1748* (Columbia, SC, 1991), 29-48.

[22]Gerald S. Graham and R.A. Humphreys (eds.), *The Navy and South America, 1807-1823: Correspondence of the Commanders-in-Chief on the South American Station* (London, 1962), xxiii-xxxiv.

activities. All contained clear anti-Spanish tendencies, but in a mercantilist world in which ships, cargoes and seafarers were rigorously categorised by nationality, pirates discriminated as little in their recruitment policies as in their choice of targets. Often mixed in nationality and race, though rarely in gender, companies of pirates from the early seventeenth century to the 1830s were generally organised along extraordinary lines. Unlike seafarers in the shipping industry, these maritime labourers were part-owners of their vessels, owned shares in the profits of their ventures, and were entitled to select (or remove) their commanders and officers. Extending such "alternative," collective principles beyond the workplace, pirate settlements were established almost in defiance of "normal" society. Thus, in locations as distant in time and space as Lundy Island and Barataria, men such as Thomas Sockwell and Jean Laffitte led pirate communities, while the fraternal tendencies of groups that styled themselves the "Confederation of Deep Sea Pirates," the "Brethren of the Coast" or the "Brethren of the Gulf" further attest to the self-conscious "otherness" of pirate life.[23]

Such brotherhoods were essentially transitory. They belonged to, and symbolized, an extraordinary business which fed off the trade and shipping of European maritime states for relatively short periods in the early modern era. With the commerce-raiders of the Islamic world from time to time preying on the same targets, the level of piratical activity in the Atlantic fluctuated dramatically. Though many factors were at play, economic forces chiefly explain this pattern.

Causalities

In the vast literature on piracy, there are numerous attempts to identify its causes. Implicit in many accounts is the notion that piracy is a product of weak and immature political, economic and social structures, that it will inevitably die out as civilization progresses. The Atlantic experience offers some support for this Whiggish interpretation, for piracy was much more prevalent before the 1730s than after and generally less of a threat as the institutions and military capabilities of states developed. But

---

[23]See Senior, *Nation of Pirates*, 30-33: Senior, "Confederation of Deep-Sea Pirates," 332; Marcus Rediker, "Hydrarchy and Libertalia: The Utopian Dimensions of Atlantic Piracy in the Early Eighteenth Century," in de Moor and van Eyck van Heslinga (eds.), *Pirates and Privateers*; Lubbock, *Cruisers, Corsairs and Slavers*, 59-72.

the outbreak of large-scale maritime lawlessness in the early nineteenth century, albeit in the context of the terminal disintegration of the Spanish Empire, tends to weaken such a thesis. Others have followed contemporaries in linking piratical activity to the cycles of war and peace, and certainly the demobilizations of 1603, 1714 and 1815 provided thousands of idle hands to do the devil's work. Yet piracy did not erupt once the peace treaties of 1748, 1763 and 1783 were signed.[24]

A further line of reasoning has looked to the unit of production – the pirate crew and community – to explain the ebb and flow of piracy. While the attractions of a libertarian lifestyle or, more important, an alternative form of social organisation may well have enticed many oppressed seafarers or political outcasts to serve under the black flag, this elucidates how a wave of piracy might be sustained rather than the reasons for its genesis.[25] Equally inadequate is the contention that piracy was precipitated by change in the political realm. This was clearly an important factor, the inter-imperial rivalries of the early modern era providing the unstable political climate in which piracy often flourished, while state policies, whether designed to nurture commercial hegemony over an area or to exclude competitors from established trades, frequently cast interlopers or rivals as pirates.[26] Yet context and definition are not the same as causality. Accordingly, to assert that the "dynamic" underlying piracy was political is to ignore the essential truth that the motive which "spurs men on to the undertaking of the most difficult Adventures is the sacred hunger of gold" – that pirates appropriated the vessels and properties of others to earn profits.[27] This might have important political ramifications, but the chief causal dynamic, as the waves of maritime lawlessness in the Atlantic demonstrate, was economic

---

[24]For instance, see Senior, "Confederation of Deep-Sea Pirates," 331-333; Rediker, *Between the Devil and the Deep Blue Sea*, 281-283; Lubbock, *Cruisers, Corsairs and Slavers*, 59.

[25]Hill, "Radical Pirates?;" Rediker, *Between the Devil and the Deep Blue Sea*, 254-287.

[26]These arguments are developed in Pérotin-Dumon, "The Pirate and the Emperor."

[27]The opening to the first published account of Sharp's buccaneering voyage of 1680, cited in Howse and Thrower (eds.), *Buccaneer's Atlas*, 1.

and was found in the forces of demand and supply which conditioned trading and shipping activity.

Analysis of these market forces suggests that some were more passive than others in instigating and sustaining piratical activity. On the demand side, pirates provided goods and services for three forms of consumer. In the first place, there is a self-satisfying element to any piratical activity and there are many instances of seafarers or others plundering vessels and goods to meet their own needs. In this sense, piracy might be viewed as demand-led, the resort of people or societies lacking basic necessities. The *boucaniers* of the early seventeenth-century Caribbean conform to this type, hunting cattle and preying upon passing ships principally for reasons of self-sufficiency.[28] While this impetus might account for some piratical attacks, it hardly explains the scale of the various waves of piracy which rippled through the Atlantic for at least a decade. During these phases, pirates undoubtedly used or destroyed some of the properties they seized. But even the most wanton, ostentatious or dissolute commerce-raider was unlikely to consume all that was taken. Prize goods surplus to requirements therefore gave rise to a market, a black market in which cheap stolen properties were purchased by merchants and dealers who generally supplied the established, respectable communities of the Atlantic world.

This second form of demand tended to sustain waves of piratical activity. Once pirates generated supplies of commodities for sale at discount prices, buyers were attracted to the entrepôts which invariably developed to handle this business. In the early seventeenth century, for instance, English and Dutch merchants regularly visited Leamcon in southern Ireland to treat with the pirate community, while traders from Leghorn, Venice, Genoa and elsewhere in the Mediterranean formed strong commercial ties with the raiders who furnished the thriving mart of Mamora in North Africa with sugar, spices, wine, cloth and a host of more mundane commodities.[29] Likewise, in the Caribbean, buccaneers and pirates were central to a transport system which saw the goods of the European maritime powers, especially Spain and her empire, redistrib-

---

[28]Cooper-Prichard, *Buccaneers*, 13-36.

[29]See John C. Appleby, "A Nursery of Pirates: The English Pirate Community in Ireland in the Early Seventeenth Century," *International Journal of Maritime History*, II, No. 1 (1990), 1-27; Senior, "Confederation of Deep-Sea Pirates."

uted within the West Indies and diverted in significant quantities to the ports of colonial North America.[30]

The services of pirates were also deployed by a third type of consumer, the state. Such demand generally arose from infant or weak authorities who lacked the resources to equip and maintain regular armed forces and therefore turned to opportunistic commerce-raiders for the military muscle they required. Again, this was not demand-led, for such employers did not establish new forces but called upon existing predatory units as a short-term solution to their deficiencies. Such a cheap option was regularly pursued in the seventeenth-century Caribbean, where buccaneers supplied much of the physical force needed by the local representatives of the British, French and Dutch states in their long war of attrition with the Spaniards.[31] A similar pragmatic arrangement pertained in the same theatre in the early nineteenth century as insurgents relied on the violence of pirates in the maritime facet of their wars of liberation. In such instances, the service provided and price agreed amounted to the same thing – the unlimited plunder of Spanish property, a goal thought to weaken the enemy as well as reward the predator. The long wave of piracy based in the Barbary regencies worked on the same premise, though here the exchange between state and commerce-raider was financial as well as military, for the corsairs generated income in the form of taxes and tributes for the littoral communities of North Africa.

While demand for the services of pirates did not initiate waves of maritime lawlessness, it played an important part in maintaining the momentum of predatory surges. Once the commercial, military or fiscal utility of piracy was demonstrated, the business might swiftly become an important, sometimes intrinsic, feature of the economic and political life of a society. This points to clear weaknesses in the structure of "normal," legal markets. Thus, pirates furnished goods and military services to communities unable to obtain sufficient, affordable supplies through prescribed mechanisms. Mediterranean markets short of northern European commodities, Spanish colonies forlornly awaiting supply vessels from Seville, North American communities obliged to purchase only British manufactures, European settlements in the Caribbean left

---

[30]Ritchie, *Captain Kidd*, 1-26.

[31]This partly explains why Bartholomew Sharp and others were acquitted of piracy on their return to London. See Howse and Thrower (eds.), *Buccaneer's Atlas*, 27-28.

unguarded due to the inadequacies of metropolitan resources, North African states impoverished by the limitations of their economic base – such were the consumers of piratical services. Of course, once legitimate traders and regular armed forces began to meet these needs, the demand for piracy fell and its practitioners were obliged to modify their operations or retire from the business.

On the supply side, piracy was only marginally conditioned by the availability of land. Bases were an important factor in that all pirates, even the most self-sufficient of marauders, needed a safe haven where vessels and crews could be replenished. While there was no shortage of such facilities in the comparatively undeveloped and sparsely populated Atlantic of the seventeenth and eighteenth centuries, the need for more substantial port amenities for the discharge of cargoes and exchange of goods might influence piratical activity. Such entrepôts emerged, of course; Leamcon, Mamora, Algiers, Sallee, Tortuga, Port Royale, the Bahamas, Madagascar, Havana, Galveston and many other places served at one time or another as pirate marts and strongholds. Though these "nests" were vulnerable to the violence of naval forces, as the reduction of Mamora in 1614, the assault on Sallee in 1637, the "cleansing" of the Bahamas in 1718, and the attack on Jean Laffitte's community at Galveston in 1821 clearly demonstrate, the pest was generally inconvenienced rather than eliminated by the measures taken.[32]

Capital requirements were more of an influence upon the level of piratical activity. Of course, such needs might be minimal, for many piracies were committed with equipment as rudimentary as the canoes and muskets used by the early *boucaniers*. Moreover, a high proportion of piratical forays were self-sustaining. In the very nature of the business, vessels, arms, stores, provisions and other necessities were taken and put to commerce-raiding, an *ad hoc* means of investment and accumulation by which more successful pirates improved and extended their capital stock at little expense. But more substantial investments were needed to mount large-scale, deep-water ventures. The funds to purchase and equip vessels, procure armaments and provisions, and recruit labour came in some cases from legitimate mercantile and government sources. For instance, the depredations of the Turkish

---

[32]See Senior, "Confederation of Deep-Sea Pirates;" Hebb, *Piracy*; Rediker, *Between the Devil and the Deep Blue Sea*, 254-287; Lubbock, *Cruisers, Corsairs and Slavers*, 59-72.

corsairs were funded by the merchants of Algiers, Sallee and other Moorish ports, while Governor Modyforde and other colonial officials invested in the buccaneering campaigns of Morgan, Sharp, Coxon and others.[33] Likewise, William Kidd's infamous cruise in the *Adventure Gally*, a privateering venture which degenerated into piracy, was funded by a consortium led by Lord Belloment, Governor of New York.[34]

On occasions, "foreign" capital was invested in piracy. In the seventeenth century, merchants in French Mediterranean ports provided funds for Barbary corsairs even as their government was negotiating ways of reducing the menace.[35] Similarly, though to a much greater degree, capital resources in the United States were deployed in the *course independante*. Vessels built for, and funds generated by, the carrying trade and privateering which American shippers successively and lucratively exploited during the Revolutionary and Naploeonic Wars, lay idle once the peace of 1814 was signed. Now prohibited from carrying for, or cruising against, the European powers, with funds and vessels surplus to the needs of home trade, American merchants and shipowners invested in potentially profitable, if dubiously legal, trading, smuggling and piratical activity in the Caribbean and South America.[36]

This was unusual, however, for capital, and land even less so, rarely precipitated surges of piracy. The supply of labour, by contrast, was invariably critical. Piracy was essentially labour intensive, with comparatively large crews required to overhaul and overwhelm prizes. Though quantitative evidence is sparse, estimates suggest that in the Jacobean era the average pirate company was over fifty strong, twice the size of the crew of an English merchantman trading in the Mediterranean

---

[33]Earle, *Corsairs of Malta and Barbary*; Gosse, *History of Piracy*, 157-158.

[34]Ritchie, *Captain Kidd*.

[35]Earle, *Corsairs of Malta and Barbary*, 15-16.

[36]Jerome R. Garitee, *The Republic's Private Navy: The American Privateering Business as Practised by Baltimore during the War of 1812* (Middletown, CT, 1977), 224-230; Howard I. Chapelle, *The History of American Sailing Ships* (New York, 1985), 238-239.

and three times that of the typical crew working in northern European waters.[37] Barbary corsairs had even more substantial complements, the larger galleys and sailing vessels carrying between 140 and 200 soldiers to board their victims.[38] In the early eighteenth century, about eighty men worked the typical pirate ships of the Caribbean and North America at a time when complements on trans-Atlantic merchantmen were falling to between fifteen and twenty men.[39] Typically, pirate crews comprised men who worked not for shipowners or the state but for themselves. They were "on the account," self-employed maritime labourers whose remuneration came from a share in the spoils. While such terms of service meant that pirates might earn windfall profits from the capture of a valuable prize, they also entailed high risks, for negative earnings would accrue from a barren sortie. This prospect of "no purchase, no pay," together with the physical danger and, most significant, the illegality of piratical work, implies that employment opportunities, or conditions of service, in more regular, secure occupations must have been lacking for labourers to turn to this hazardous work.[40]

Such flaws in the labour market were at the root of the business of piracy in the Atlantic during the early modern era. Underlying each wave of lawlessness were discrepancies between the demand for, and supply of, labour. In some instances, the weakness was chronic and broadly based, and a steady flow of pirate recruits was forthcoming for long periods. The persistence and extent of Barbary piracy, for example, was in many ways symptomatic of the unemployment, underemployment and widespread poverty which characterised the economies of the North African regencies. Though the immediate hinterlands of Algiers, Tunis and Tripoli were relatively fertile and productive, it was the sea and commerce-raiding which provided manufactures, raw materials and slaves for distribution through a trading network which extended

---

[37]Senior, *Nation of Pirates*, 30; Ralph Davis, *The Rise of the English Shipping Industry in the Seventeenth and Eighteenth Centuries* (London, 1962), 110.

[38]Earle, *Corsairs of Malta and Barbary*, 53.

[39]Rediker, *Between the Devil and the Deep Blue Sea*, 265; Davis, *English Shipping Industry*, 111.

[40]Similar prospects faced privateersmen. See David J. Starkey, *British Privateering Enterprise in the Eighteenth Century* (Exeter, 1990).

throughout the Islamic world.⁴¹ In the very different setting of the early seventeenth-century Caribbean, a similar pattern was evident. The infant economies of the region, hindered by Spain's monopolistic policies, could not employ the miscellany of Europeans who gravitated towards the fabled wealth of the Americas. As cattle-hunting *boucaniers* evolved into commerce-raiding buccaneers, so the development of large-scale sugar plantations intensified the chronic over-supply of labour by squeezing a veritable class of smallholders off the land. Piratical forays were one solution to this crisis and over time a necessary search for sustenance became not only a viable business but also a way of life.⁴²

Exacerbating these market inefficiencies in the Caribbean were similar problems in Europe. In England, Spain, France and elsewhere, the late sixteenth and early seventeenth centuries were marked by rapid population growth and economic stagnation, a combination which led to high and sustained levels of unemployment. Together with the political and religious crises of the period, this helped fuel the flow of emigrants to the New World, thereby adding to the over-supply of labour and the wave of buccaneering it generated. It was also a factor contributing to the short wave of piracy which originated in Jacobean England in the early seventeenth century. Though evidence relating to the occupational background of those engaged in this wave of piracy is sparse, it would seem that a sizeable proportion, perhaps as large as thirty percent, of the pirate population was drawn from land-based occupations. While a number, like J.M. Barrie's aptly-named "Gentleman" Starkey,⁴³ came from the professions and the ranks of the well-to-do, there were artisans, husbandmen and even a poet among those who sailed with the "Confederation of Deep Sea Pirates."⁴⁴ The inference to be drawn from such data is that high and chronic levels of unemployment in the domestic economy encouraged some to seek a livelihood in lawless activity at sea.

More central to the outbreak of short waves of piracy was over-supply in the seafaring labour market. This was a large, diverse market

---

⁴¹Earle, *Corsairs of Malta and Barbary*.

⁴²Bridenbaugh and Bridenbaugh, *No Peace Beyond the Line*, 175-176.

⁴³"Gentleman Starkey, once an usher in a public school, and still dainty in his ways of killing." J.M. Barrie, *Peter Pan* (1911; reprint, London, 1992), 173.

⁴⁴Senior, "Confederation of Deep-Sea Pirates."

in which labour was procured by shipowners in exchange for wages. It was notable for its fluctuations, a trait directly linked to the cycle of war and peace. But in meeting the demands of the navy and privateers in wartime, generally aided by state intervention, the seafaring labour market tended to generate a capacity difficult to maintain in peacetime, leading on occasion to outbreaks of lawlessness. This pattern is clear in the English market for seafarers in the early seventeenth century.[45] Largely as a result of the war against Spain, which formally commenced in 1585, the number of seafarers engaged in English naval, privateering and merchant vessels increased from an estimated 16,000 in the early 1580s to nearly 50,000 in the last years of Elizabeth's reign.[46] When naval demobilisation and the suspension of letters of marque occurred suddenly in the summer of 1603, a large proportion of the maritime workforce was rendered idle. This acute crisis, together with the chronic shortage of work in the economy as a whole, meant that relatively few sailors could obtain employment ashore or afloat. Contemporaries readily recognised the piratical implications of such a situation, officials in numerous English port towns warning the central authorities of the threat to law, order and property posed by the "great number of sailors, mariners and other masterless men that heretofore have been at sea in men-of-war."[47] And, of course, once the efficacy and rewards of predatory activity were demonstrated, the urge to prey upon trade gathered a momentum of its own and the wave of piracy was sustained by new recruits and by prizes taken in a widening operational theatre.

A similar pattern can be detected a century or so later. The demand for seafarers in the long wars of 1689-1714, the first Anglo-French struggle to assume truly global proportions, was unprecedented. In France, the manning requirements of the great fleets of Louis XIV were immense, while in this era of Jean Bart, de Forbin and *l'apogee de la course* a considerable number of seafarers were recruited

---

[45]David J. Starkey, "War and the Market for Seafarers in Britain, 1736-1792," in Lewis R. Fischer and Helge W. Nordvik (eds.), *Shipping and Trade 1750-1950: Essays in Maritime Economic History* (Pontefract, 1990), 25-42.

[46]Senior, "Confederation of Deep-Sea Pirates," 331.

[47]Senior, *Nation of Pirates*; Senior, "Confederation of Deep-Sea Pirates."

by privateering *armateurs*.⁴⁸ Likewise, in England and the United Provinces the navy exerted substantial pressure on the market for seafarers, with almost 50,000 men serving in Queen Anne's fleets in the closing years of the war. At the same time, the irregular buccaneering forces which had harassed and plundered Spanish trade before the war were now given the authority to continue their business as privateers and, moreover, to add a significant anti-French or anti-English string to their bows. But on the cessation of hostilities, a by now familiar pattern can be observed. Navies demobilised – within a year, the British navy had cut its workforce to under 14,000 – privateering came to an end, and a large body of seamen were left without work.⁴⁹ And large-scale seafaring unemployment, as contemporaries noted, especially in the Caribbean and North America, where buccaneers-turned-privateersmen were left idle, bred the piratical wave which ensued in the years following the peace of Utrecht. With wage reductions and harsher terms of service – those companions of unemployment – also featuring strongly during this period, a flow of recruits to the black flag was forthcoming for the next decade or so.⁵⁰

Labour surpluses also underpinned the *course independante* of the early nineteenth century. Again, the end of a long war with an important privateering dimension led to unemployment and, as a century earlier, the bulk of over-capacity was located in the Caribbean.⁵¹ At the same time, the rapid expansion in the carrying, privateering and shipping interests of the US, which had generated so much maritime capital in the French Revolutionary and Napoleonic conflicts, was mirrored in the growth of the seafaring labour force. With the dismantling in 1815 of the hothouse in which this American enterprise had flourished, seafarers, as well as ships and funds, were relatively abundant in Baltimore, New York, Boston and other northern ports. In such a context, the profitable

---

⁴⁸Ernest H. Jenkins, *A History of the French Navy from its Beginnings to the Present Day* (London, 1973); J.S. Bromley, "The French Privateering War, 1702-1713" in Bromley (ed.), *Corsairs and Navies*, 231-242.

⁴⁹Christopher C. Lloyd, *The British Seaman, 1200-1860: A Social Survey* (London, 1968), 286-287.

⁵⁰Rediker, *Between the Devil and the Deep Blue Sea*, 254-287.

⁵¹Lubbock, *Cruisers, Corsairs and Slavers*, 59-61.

potential of the uncertain political and commercial situation in the Caribbean attracted a flow of surplus maritime resources from New England and the Middle States to the West Indies and South America.[52] This flow of Baltimore schooners and American seafarers, together with the picaroons of former Spanish and French privateersmen, contributed significantly to the *course independante* and the wars of liberation.

While the short waves of piracy were largely a consequence of market deficiencies, such conditions did not persist. Pirates might have supplied communities with goods and provisions, and colonies with military services, for a number of years, but theirs was essentially a short-term business.[53] In all instances, it was only a matter of time before "regular" merchants and the state began to encroach on the pirates by providing competitive, legitimate services and by using the law to criminalise those who dealt with pirates.[54] While such measures reduced the demand for piratical services, attempts were made to cut the supply of recruits to this labour-intensive activity. Thus, the violence of the courts and the navy were deployed to eliminate pirates and to deter would-be volunteers, and pardons were offered to make gamekeepers out of poachers. But the main precipitant of maritime lawlessness – the supply of labour – was also its main constraint. In this, the business of piracy provides an unusual vantage point from which to consider the efficiency of the market for seafarers.

Piracy and the Efficiency of the Market for Seafarers

The various waves of piracy which swept the Atlantic in the early modern era were essentially a function of economic factors, chief among these being disequilibria between supply and demand in the labour market. While the long waves reflected chronic deficiencies in the underdeveloped economies of the Caribbean and North Africa, the short waves were causally related to the oversupply in the market for seafarers at the end of war in 1603, 1714 and 1815. This latter conclusion, in

---

[52]Garitee, *Republic's Private Navy*, 224-230.

[53]This is symbolized in the inclusion of a timepiece in pirate flags of the early eighteenth century. See Rediker, *Between the Devil and the Deep Blue Sea*, 278-281.

[54]See Senior, "Confederation of Deep-Sea Pirates."

particular, tends to support the notion that the seafaring labour market in the age of sail exhibited many aspects of inefficiency.[55]

Yet this is not to suggest that the market was inherently defective. Significantly, piratical waves were comparatively brief, lasting from ten to twenty years. In each case, piracy reached its peak some years after the onset of peace.[56] While state violence generally hastened the end, the operation of the labour market was largely responsible for the demise of these waves of piracy. In postwar years, unemployment, wage reductions and harsher conditions of service may have encouraged large numbers of seafarers to go "on the account," but it persuaded many more to leave the sea altogether and deterred others from seeking employment afloat. Over time, the labour surplus cleared. As the supply of seafarers largely conditioned the supply of pirates this return to equilibrium curtailed the flow of potential freebooters. Accordingly, once pirate crews were depleted by death, retirement and the courts, a shortage of replacement labour made the productive unit less effective and the business entered a downward spiral. That it took at least a decade to complete this piratical cycle suggests that the market was slow to re-adjust to "normal" conditions rather than perpetually inefficient.

Moreover, lawless surges were not always evident in the aftermath of maritime conflicts, as the relative calm following the great imperial struggles of 1739-1748, 1756-1763 and 1776-1783 testify. Two inter-related factors explain this differential pattern. First, the symbiotic relationship between trade and shipping was seriously disrupted by wars, which spawned short waves of piracy. In each instance, the expansion of shipping was disproportionate to the level of trade in particular regions of the Atlantic. Accordingly, in England the three-fold expansion in the seafaring labour force of the late sixteenth and early seventeenth centuries was linked to the major and unprecedented growth of privateering, which emerged as "the characteristic form of maritime warfare" in the period.[57] Likewise, in the Caribbean the long wars of 1689-1714 boosted predatory activity and maritime resources but depressed

---

[55]Kindleberger, *Mariners and Markets*, 90.

[56]The cyclical pattern of piracy is apparent in Senior, *Nation of Pirates*; and Rediker, *Between the Devil and the Deep Blue Sea*.

[57]Kenneth R. Andrews, *Elizabethan Privateering: English Privateering during the Spanish War, 1585-1603* (Cambridge, 1964), 6.

aggregate levels of trade. And in the northern ports of the United States, the windfall profits of neutrality and privateering rather than any expansion in domestic imports and exports stimulated the extraordinary growth in shipping which marked the years 1793-1814.[58] With the end of each war, the "artificial" conditions which had stimulated the expansion of shipping – privateering or neutrality – swiftly evaporated and a surplus of shipping resources, especially labour, remained.

At such junctures, a second factor, the depressed level of foreign trade, ensured that an adequate transfer of resources from belligerent to commercial employment did not occur. Again, this was evident in each case. While sluggish growth characterised English overseas commerce in the early seventeenth century, and the British imperial system from the 1690s to the 1740s, it was also a feature of the US economy in the decades after Waterloo.[59] The situation in the mid-eighteenth century was rather different. While privateering was a prominent feature of the mid-century wars, it was significant only during short phases of these conflicts and was conducted while trade proceeded, and in a number of cases flourished.[60] Moreover, in each of the post-war eras – 1749-1755, 1764-1775 and 1784-1793 – transatlantic commerce boomed so that the demands placed on European shipping were sufficient to absorb enough resources, including labour, to obviate any major disequilibrium in the seafaring labour market. In other words, the divergence between shipping and trade in the wars of the mid-eighteenth century was never wide enough to foster large-scale unemployment and its child, piracy.

Insofar as piracy was a barometer of labour market efficiency, this implies that the market functioned relatively well in postwar years from the 1740s to the 1790s, but at other times was much slower to adjust to the dislocations of war.[61] It also offers a new perspective on the argument that the eradication of piracy in the eighteenth century

---

[58]Ralph Davis, "English Foreign Trade, 1700-1774," *Economic History Review*, XV (1962), 285-303; Garitee, *Republic's Private Navy*.

[59]Davis, "English Foreign Trade;" Garitee, *Republic's Private Navy*.

[60]Starkey, *British Privateering Enterprise*.

[61]Starkey, "War and the Market for Seafarers."

contributed significantly to productivity gains in shipping.[62] On the contrary, it would seem that it was the relative efficiency of the commercial and shipping markets that largely explains why piracy was much less prevalent in the Atlantic after the 1720s.

---

[62]James F. Shepherd and Gary M. Walton, *Shipping, Maritime Trade and the Economic Development of Colonial North America* (Cambridge, 1972).

"Advance Notes" and the Recruitment of Maritime Labour in Britain in the Nineteenth Century

David M. Williams

That wage levels are a crucial factor in any labour market is obvious enough. What is less evident is the impact of how wages are paid. Yet the nature and supply of labour are clearly influenced by the form of payment, whether by time (hour, day, week or longer) or the piece, following the completion of agreed tasks or services in small or large units. Forms of payment depend on many elements, notably the character and context of the labour involved and the customary practice that evolved over time. In the age of sail, seafaring labour was paid in various ways, with differences arising from the specific character of the work undertaken.[1] In whaling and some fisheries, labour was paid by the "lay," receiving a share in the returns of a voyage; a similar form of remuneration prevailed on privateers. Payment by the piece, in this instance the voyage, was the usual practice on other fishing vessels and in short-sea trades — in the case of Britain, for instance, coastal shipping (especially the coal trade from the northeast to London) and on nearby European routes.[2] But many seafarers in the merchant service were paid by the month at a rate (which often varied according to destination) agreed at the time of enlistment. Still, many merchant seamen, particu-

---

[1]On the payment of seamen, see Ralph Davis, *The Rise of the English Shipping Industry in the Seventeenth and Eighteenth Centuries* (2nd ed., Newton Abbott, 1972), 133-158; Jon Press, "Wages in the Merchant Navy, 1815-54," *Journal of Transport History*, 3rd series, II (1981), 37-52.

[2]While payment by the voyage was usually confined to relatively short trades, there are examples from the 1860s of seamen in some North Atlantic trades being paid this way. See Judith Fingard, "'Those Crimps of Hell and Goblins Damned': The Image and Reality of Quebec's Sailortown Bosses," in Rosemary Ommer and Gerald Panting (eds.), *Working Men Who Got Wet* (St. John's, 1980), 328-329.

larly those engaged for long overseas voyages, were in a sense piece workers, paid on completion based on the duration of the voyage at the agreed rate.

While the level and form of returns to labour were clearly crucial influences on the labour market, the timing of the payment was also significant. Seamen, compared with most types of labour, were exceptional in that many were paid irregularly, at the completion of voyages after months or even years of service. But while such recompense came at the termination of employment, seamen were also often paid in advance for part of their labour. Such payments might be in cash or in the form of an "advance note." In Scandinavia and the Baltic advances were in cash, while in France, Belgium, the Netherlands and Germany notes were more common.[3] In Britain, advances were invariably in the form of notes.

The advance note is the subject of this study. The approach is to consider first the nature and function of advance notes. Second, we will examine the consequences of the system. Third, we will see why notes became a subject of increasing concern in the nineteenth century and how government came to investigate and act on the matter. Finally, we will consider the significance of advance notes in the context of "mariners and markets" in the second half of the nineteenth century.

At the outset it is appropriate to explain the function of the advance note. A statement by J. O'Dowd, Assistant Solicitor of the Board of Customs, before the Royal Commission on Unseaworthy Ships in 1874 described notes as follows:

> The shipowners at the several ports of the United Kingdom have felt it necessary to give seamen engaged for their ships an advance for every voyage of not less than a month's wage, to enable them to pay debts contracted for board and lodging ashore while waiting employment, and for the purchase of clothes and outfit requisite for the voyage. This is done, not by a money payment, but by an advance note...delivered to the seamen generally signed by the shipping master at the

---

[3]*Nautical Magazine*, August 1875, quoted in Thomas Brassey, *British Seamen* (London, 1877), 201.

port at the time the seamen sign the ship's articles in the presence of that officer.[4]

O'Dowd's statement is an admirable starting point but it contains implications which require qualification. First, his comments suggest that advance notes were peculiar to Britain; as well, they convey the notion that notes were of relatively recent origin. Neither is correct. Advance notes were a feature found throughout the world wherever there was a significant demand for seamen. They were used in other European and North American ports, and particularly in Québec, Australia, and India.[5] Hence, although my focus is on Britain, many facets have a significance for international maritime labour markets. Moreover, the practice of granting advances was long-standing. Ralph Davis provides evidence of them in certain trades from the mid-seventeenth century, and a 1744 statement by Bristol merchants reveals established practice:

> It has been always a custom to advance a month's wages to all the men intended to be ship (except the chief mate) either to discharge the debt contracted to the landlord with whom they lodge or to fitt themselves with cloths and necessary for the voyage.[6]

A further qualification to O'Dowd's submission is the reference to "an advance for every voyage." This was not the case: advances were only given to seamen signing-on for a voyage likely to be of considerable duration. The coastal, Irish and short-sea trades, where voyages lasted at most a few weeks, did not follow the practice. Notes were reserved for the most part for trades outside European waters, although they were

---

[4]Great Britain, Parliament, House of Commons, *Parliamentary Papers (BPP)*, "Royal Commission on Unseaworthy Ships," 1873 [853], XXXVI, appendix XXX.

[5]Québec was notorious in this respect because its pattern of trade and the need for crews for newly constructed vessels led to a pressing demand. High wages and generous advances were the result, with the latter used to lure seamen from other vessels. See Judith Fingard, *Jack in Port: Sailortowns of Eastern Canada* (Toronto, 1982).

[6]Walter E. Minchinton (ed.), *The Trade of Bristol in the Eighteenth Century* (Bristol, 1957), 153, quoted in Davis, *English Shipping Industry*, 143.

also found in the Baltic and Mediterranean trades.[7] It was thus deep-water trades where the advance note was most common. It follows that certain ports – depending on their trading patterns – were more likely to use advance notes. London and west coast ports, such as Glasgow, Liverpool and Cardiff, used notes far more widely than east coast ports, where established coastal routes and close European connections characterized trade. Advance notes were generally confined to large ports with sizeable local markets for maritime labour that had a significant involvement in long-distance trades. In Liverpool, for example, the note was so customary that a witness before an 1878 Select Committee observed that "the thing has got to be so much as custom that whether he [the seamen] wants it or not, I believe he takes it."[8] Still, just as the note was rare in some trades and ports, only some owners issued notes. It is important to remember when considering comments and criticisms that shipowners' views reflected their particular situations.

It is clear then that the advance note was extensively used in long-distance trades and most fully developed in major ports.[9] Perhaps the clearest evidence of its widespread employment – although this anticipates future discussion – is that, following abolition by government, notes had to be offered to secure labour for long-distance sail trades and were eventually legalized anew. The system dated at least to the seventeenth century but, despite such long-standing origins, the bulk of evidence on advance notes is to be found in the second half of the nineteenth century, particularly from the 1860s, when they became a matter of considerable debate.[10] The timing is not without significance,

---

[7]Davis, *English Shipping Industry*, 133, writing on the seventeenth and eighteenth centuries, includes Baltic, Russian, Iberian and Mediterranean routes among the "longer voyages." The growing frequency of deep-water trades and possibly some reduction in voyage times provided a new perspective on "long distance trades."

[8]*BPP*, "Select Committee on Merchant Seamen Bill," 1878 [205], XVI, qq. 748, 1786-1798.

[9]It is hoped that access to the Atlantic Canada Shipping Project's one percent sample of non-Canadian British Empire crew agreements will, in due course, permit a more precise indication of the extent of usage and changes over time.

[10]Not all those who commented on notes in the mid-nineteenth century appreciated the longevity of the practice. For example, E.A. Arthur, a surveyor with American Lloyds, was of the view that notes had been in existence "at least thirty years;" see *BPP*,

for in the mid-nineteenth century discussion of any aspect of shipping embodied the sail/steam dimension. Many who commented on advance notes observed that they were confined largely to sail because steam voyages were of relatively short duration and steam liners employed seamen on a much more regular basis.[11] Such observations underscore the traditional purpose and context of advance notes and emphasise that they were peculiar to the age of sail.

Having established this, it is now pertinent to enquire how the system worked in practice and what its consequences were. An example provided by O'Dowd in 1874 illustrates the form and practice.

> Ten days after the departure of the ship...from the last port or place in the River or Firth of Clyde, in which from any cause she may be before finally leaving for the voyage for which this note is issued, pay to the order of (seamen's name) the sum of £3.17.s.6d., provided the said seamen sails in and continues in the said vessel and daily earns his wages according to agreement.
>
> (Signed) ROBERT DOUGLAS, Master.
> To Messrs. Henderson and Co.
> Hope Street, Glasgow[12]

The above case reveals a number of features that deserve emphasis, including the fact that advance payment was made not in money but in the form of a promissory note to be paid only if the seamen sailed in the vessel and after such time as the voyage could be said to have properly begun. So there could be no doubt about the

---

"Royal Commission on Unseaworthy Ships," 1874 [1027-I], XXXIV, qq. 15,370-15,371.

[11]*BPP*, "Royal Commission on Unseaworthy Ships," 1874, [1027-I] XXXIV, qq. 10,589-10,590; *BPP*, "Select Committee on the Merchant Seamen Bill," 1878 [205], XVI, qq. 680, 753, 1740-1746, 4292, 4365, 4404-4410; *BPP*, "Royal Commission on Loss of Life at Sea," 1884-1885 [4577], XXXV, qq. 20,647-20,662.

[12]*BPP*, "Royal Commission on Unseaworthy Ships," 1873, [853], XXXVI, appendix XXX.

"proper" commencement of a voyage, the note defined the term.[13] Moreover, to take account of eventualities, such as seamen who managed to desert soon after sailing or vessels forced to return to port after a few days at sea, payment was not made until ten days after departure, although the precise conditions varied from port to port. For example, London notes were payable three days after the ship cleared Deal, while Cardiff notes were payable three days after leaving the docks.[14] Although this became rarer toward the end of the nineteenth century, notes were sometimes given for an advance of two months pay.[15]

While in theory notes were sensible, recognising the peculiar features of seafaring labour and providing a legal safeguard for the risks incurred by shipowners, in reality they embodied significant dangers. These lay in the fact that for a note to be used by a seaman to acquire goods or services, he had to induce someone to advance money or credit on it. Moreover, any party who advanced money against an advance note — and thereby incurred a risk — had an obvious interest in ensuring that the promise of service was kept. From these two basic features a host of potential abuses could follow. The cashing of a note put cash or credit in the hands of seamen who were free to use it for any purpose and not necessarily to cover outfitting, lodging debts or family provision. Drink and riotous living were held to be (and probably were) the chief items of expenditure. A more obvious and real abuse was that a seaman, having cashed his note, might not sail and hence the note would be dishonoured. Such action would represent a breach of contract between the seamen and his employer and a fraud against whoever had advanced money or goods against it. Such risks ensured that money would be advanced only at a

---

[13]The instance quoted included both the "River" and "Firth" of Forth — so there could be no legal quibbling over geographic terms by shrewd Scots lawyers!

[14]On London, see *BPP*, "Royal Commission on Unseaworthy Ships," 1874 [1027-I], XXXIV, qq. 13,370-13,371. On Cardiff, see *ibid.*, qq. 1764-1769, especially q. 1766, where Thomas Snow Miller, Collector of Customs in Cardiff, described attempts to get the customary period extended to ten days but, no doubt due to the influence of crimps, "masters could not get hands on these terms."

[15]It has been suggested that notes were customarily given for two months pay and in some instances for three months. See Conrad Dixon, "The Rise and Fall of the Crimp, 1840-1914," in Stephen Fisher (ed.), *British Shipping and Seamen, 1630-1960: Some Studies* (Exeter, 1984), 49-67. My own reading of the evidence for the mid-nineteenth century suggests that one month's pay was the standard advance.

discount of anywhere from five to forty percent.[16] Persons who advanced money were generally associated with the avowed purpose of notes: suppliers of kit — usually referred to as tailors or outfitters — and boarding house keepers who specialised in catering for seafarers (crimps). Sailors' Homes, following their establishment from the 1830s also discounted notes — at much lower rates — but crimps were the principal handlers.[17] Invariably, outfitters and boarding house keepers worked together and sometimes the functions were combined. Often such individuals were actively involved in the supply of seamen to outgoing vessels and were likely to have found the seamen his new berth. Parties who made an advance against a note had a very obvious interest in making sure, by any means possible, that the seaman joined his ship. Hence, these individuals endeavoured to keep control of the seamen until such time as he could be delivered to his vessel. Providing drink and low company were the best means to ensure this and an escort of the crimp's associates — together with some "ladies of the town" to lighten proceedings — served to guarantee it, thereby safeguarding the investment.

Such were the inherent features of the advance note that opened the door to abuse and corruption. Malpractice arising from the notes was the order of the day, according to nineteenth-century commentators. Contemporaries also noted a flood of further deplorable features.[18] Notes, it was said, encouraged seamen to be feckless, recklessly getting through all the earnings of a previous voyage in the knowledge that they

---

[16]Ten percent was the most commonly admitted rate of discount but this has a notional, nominal character about it; invariably, the supply of over-priced goods and services raised the real rate far higher. A rate of fifty percent was suggested by the MP, Henry Labouchere in a Commons debate in 1850. *Hansard's Parliamentary Debates,* 11 February 1850.

[17]On sailors' homes, see Alston Kennerly, "Seamen's Missions and Sailor's Homes: Spiritual and Social Welfare Provisions in British Ports in the Nineteenth Century," in Stephen Fisher (ed.), *Studies in British Privateering, Trading Enterprises and Seamen's Welfare, 1770-1900* (Exeter, 1987), 121-165. On rates, see Sarah B. Palmer, "Seamen Ashore in Late Nineteenth Century London: Protection from the Crimps," in Paul Adam (ed.), *Seamen in Society* (Paris, 1980), 62-63. Sailors' homes sometimes discounted notes to their cost. See *BPP,* "Select Committee on the Merchant Seamen Bill," 1878 [205], XVI, qq. 3336-3344.

[18]This paragraph draws on arguments repeated regularly in all the various official enquiries and contemporary literature cited throughout this paper.

could fall back on an advance. Again, dishonest seamen could acquire notes with no intention of sailing. Above all, notes were seen as a factor determining the pattern of labour recruitment for long-distance voyages. Effectively, notes – or rather their discounting, which was what gave rise to profit – encouraged certain parties to seek berths on behalf of seamen. Crimps and boarding house keepers gained the "permission" of seamen to secure contracts on their behalf through providing facilities for drink and "a good time," thereby encouraging debt. Seamen naturally responded to such incentives, in the process promoting an unhealthy recruitment system as well as access to drink, which allegedly led to debauchery and moral weakness. In short, notes placed seamen in the hands of dubious and often criminal operators and rendered them open to corruption and exploitation. The unscrupulous behaviour of crimps, desirous of ensuring that their "investments" boarded ship, often led to seamen joining vessels in an unfit condition. There were safety implications in this and even more so on those occasions when crimps endeavoured to safeguard their investment by providing "substitutes" who might have no seafaring skills or experience and might literally be picked up on the street. Crew discipline and morale were also jeopardized by disgruntled seamen who knew that their first, and sometimes second, month of labour (referred to by seamen as "the dead horse") was effectively without reward.[19] There was a danger too that seamen, in the opening months of an engagement when they had no accumulated wages to lose, might desert. This was common when vessels called at ports in the early stages of a voyage or visited New York, Québec, San Francisco and other high wage ports. These observations need to be viewed in their context, but while the extent of abuse may be in question, there can be no doubt that it occurred, probably on a wide scale.

Advance notes appear to have been of no concern until the second quarter of the nineteenth century. This may have been because the practice became more widespread from around 1800, as long-distance trades, where notes were given, grew rapidly. North Atlantic trades expanded greatly due to the growth of the Anglo-USA connection, particularly in cotton, and the expansion of the emigrant and British North American timber trades. Further developments included the growth of South American routes, new opportunities in the east following the abolition of the East India Company's monopoly, and the beginnings of

---

[19]Dixon, "The Rise and Fall," 56.

commerce with Australasia. Yet while such expansion promoted the use of advance notes, other factors brought them under public scrutiny. From the 1830s, shipping assumed a much wider profile in political, economic and social debate in Britain.[20] Issues such as the strength of the British mercantile marine and the repeal of the Navigation Laws; safety at sea; the discipline, morals and welfare of seafarers; and the quality and supply of seamen all commanded attention. In each area the advance note emerged as a relevant feature. The first such official instance was probably the 1835 investigation by the Select Committee on the Causes of Shipwrecks, which touched on abuses of "advances of wages."[21] Fifteen years later, the Mercantile Marine Act of 1850 included clauses dealing with advances.[22]

In the 1860s and 1870s, for a variety of reasons maritime issues assumed even greater prominence. First, there was a heightening of the long-standing interest in the condition and welfare of seamen, as witnessed by the activities of reformers such as Toynbee, Ryder, Leach and Dixon, and the Society for Improving the Condition of Merchant Seamen, which prompted a spate of publications and much debate.[23] In addition, the safety issue gained huge prominence because of Plimsoll's campaign against "unseaworthy ships;" while the focus of that crusade was the loading and condition of vessels, the nature and quality of seamen also came up. At the same time, the late 1860s and early 1870s were significant in the more general relations between workers and

---

[20]On these general issues, see Sarah Palmer, *Politics, Shipping and the Repeal of the Navigation Laws* (Manchester, 1990); Conrad Dixon, "Legislation and the Sailors' Lot," in Adam (ed.), *Seamen in Society*, 96-106; David M. Williams, "The Quality, Skill and Supply of Maritime Labour: Causes of Concern in Britain, 1850-1914," in Lewis R. Fischer, *et al.* (eds.), *The North Sea. Twelve Essays on the Social History of Maritime Labour* (Stavanger, 1992), 41-58.

[21]*BPP*, "Select Committee into the Causes of Shipwrecks," 1836 [567], XVII, ix.

[22]13 and 14 Victoria, c. 93, s. 60. The act aimed to regulate advance notes by requiring them to be made before a shipping master on prescribed forms. This did not work and was repealed in 1854 in the Merchant Shipping Act, 17 and 18 Vict., c. 104.

[23]On campaigns over seamen's welfare in the mid-nineteenth century, see David M. Williams, "Mid-Victorian Attitudes to Seamen and Maritime Reform: The Society for Improving the Condition of Merchant Seamen, 1867," *International Journal of Maritime History*, III (1991), 101-126.

employers. Laws such as the Master and Servant Act of 1867 and the Criminal Law Amendment Act of 1871 – both hostile to labour in the matter of contracts – and, following the agitation that these provoked, the more equitable Employer and Workman Act and the Conspiracy and Protection of Property Act, both of 1875, encouraged consideration of the special circumstances that surrounded contracts between seamen and shipowners.[24] The consequence of these varied forces was a veritable flood of enquiries, publications and debate, both public and private. Merely to mention official investigations in the decade of the 1870s illustrates the high level of concern. In 1873 there was the Report of the Assistant Secretary, Marine Department, with reference to the supply of merchant seamen; sitting in the same year and in 1874 was the Royal Commission on Unseaworthy Ships and in 1878 came the Select Committee on the Merchant Seamen's Bill. In addition there were a series of Consular reports on British seamen. In all such inquiries and reports the issue of advances loomed large.

Such was the extent of the debate that any attempt to recount it in full is beyond the scope of this paper. But the gist can be conveyed relatively succinctly.[25] Almost to a man, those who considered advance notes condemned them. "The advance note is the root of all evil amongst sailors," argued the President of the Cardiff Chamber of Commerce.[26] James O'Dowd claimed that "of all the evils connected with merchant shipping, the very worst is the advance note."[27] "One great cause of the deterioration of our sailors appears to me to be the system now prevalent of giving advances to men," Thomas Brassey observed, continuing that "the issue of advance notes to seamen on engagement is a matter of

---

[24]On labour legislation generally, see R.Y. Hedges and A. Winterbottom, *The Legal History of Trade Unionism* (London, 1930).

[25]The best summary of contemporary views is Brassey, *British Seamen*, 178-211. This study, as the author acknowledged, was based almost exclusively on "Recent parliamentary and official documents."

[26]*BPP*, "Royal Commission on Unseaworthy Ships," 1873 [853], XXXVI, qq. 8285 and 8449, evidence of Colonel E.S. Hill.

[27]*Ibid.*, q. 8570.

general complaint."[28] One witness before the Select Committee on the Merchant Seamen Bill even asserted that notes were "mischievous in every respect."[29] Underlying such condemnations were the basic arguments: that notes "encouraged drunkenness and debauchery" and "placed seamen in the hands of crimps," who "put them aboard intoxicated" thereby endangering safety; led to "the defraudment of seamen;" "encouraged the recruitment of a 'lower class' of seamen;" were responsible for "demoralisation;" and provided an incentive to desert in foreign ports. In addition to such long-standing criticisms, there were newer diatribes contending that recent provisions that permitted seamen (who might have received advances) to protest against serving in allegedly "unseaworthy ships" could give rise to fraudulent and false claims. There were also legal questions associated with the commencement of a contract, clearly vital where advance notes were concerned. Did a contract commence when the seaman signed-on; when he received an advance note; when the note was cashed; or when he "joined the ship," a concept which provides its own definitional problems?

Many of these issues came to the fore in the proceedings of the Select Committee on the Merchant Seamen Bill of 1878. The complexities are revealed in an answer by Courtenay Peregrine Ilbert, the civil servant responsible for drafting the bill. In response to a question on a particular clause, Ilbert replied that:

> under existing law, if a seaman obtains an advance... and then breaks his contract and does not join ship, he may be punished; he may be sent to prison for neglecting or refusing to join; but the Bill proposes to repeal so much of the existing law as impose penalties for refusing to join. The consequences would be that, with regard to a seamen who obtained an advance, and then absconded, although he would be subject to a civil liability for breach of contract, yet it would be difficult to hit him under any provision of criminal law. I speak with some diffidence...but it appears...that there is no provision of

---

[28]Brassey, *British Seamen*, 187-188.

[29]*BPP*, "Select Committee on the Merchant Seamen Bill," 1878 [205], XVI, qq. 1786-1798.

> the criminal law...which...would clearly apply...The offence would not be embezzlement, it would not be larceny, and it would hardly be obtaining money under false pretences. Therefore, it was thought advisable to impose a penalty for breach of contract committed under these circumstances, which, in fact, amount to fraud.[30]

The above reveals clearly the legal niceties associated with the advance note and the failure to meet its obligations. If we add that under the Merchant Shipping Act of 1854 a seamen "neglecting or refusing without reasonable cause to join his ship" was liable to a forfeit of wages and imprisonment, with or without hard labour, while the terms of the 1878 Bill left "neglecting to join" (however that might be defined) as liable to civil remedy, the complexities of the legal position and the wisdom of pursuing them no further here is only too apparent.[31]

For such reasons, opinion was firmly against the advance note. No one really argued for it, although there were those who stressed its original purpose of financing outfits. There were others who, while sharing in the condemnation, argued that it was not a matter for official action since the practice was freely negotiated between employers and workers and shipowners had the power to end the system if they chose.[32] The vast majority of people – and the official reports of 1874 and 1878 – believed that advance notes should be abolished. Yet there were a host of reservations. Many shipowners claimed that advances were crucial to the recruitment of seamen for long-distance voyages in sail and that without them seamen would not be forthcoming. Again it was suggested that some seamen did use advances for their avowed

---

[30]*Ibid.*, XVI, q. 7.

[31]The 1854 act can be found in 17 & 18 Vict., c. 104, while the 1878 bill is formally titled "Bill to amend the Law relating to Merchant Seamen," *BPP*, 1878 [79], V, 125.

[32]Significantly, such views were held by Thomas Gray and Thomas Farrer, long-serving Board of Trade officials who were strong supporters of free markets. See David M. Williams, "State Regulation of Merchant Shipping 1839-1894: The Bulk Carrying Trades," in Sarah B. Palmer and Glyndwr Williams (eds.), *Charted and Uncharted Waters* (London, 1982), 55-80; Dixon, "The Rise and Fall," 58-59. Gray recommended to the 1885 Royal Commission that advance notes be legalised again; *BPP*, "Royal Commission on Loss of Life at Sea," 1884-1885 [4577], XXXV, qq. 20,693-20,718.

purpose of purchasing necessary kit (and the special cases of the shipwrecked sailors and foreign seamen arriving in Britain seeking work were sometimes advanced), while other mariners, even more virtuous, availed themselves of advances to make provision for dependants.[33] In response, opponents argued that if advances were necessary for recruitment, why not then make them in cash which in theory would remove seamen from the clutches of crimps? Alternatively, some suggested that all ships should carry "slop chests" to enable mariners to purchase necessary kit aboard. To cater for dependants, why not provide allotment notes at regular intervals? Yet none of these suggestions really solved the problems. Cash advances hardly guaranteed to protect seamen from crimps; indeed, cash was even more attractive to them and riskier for shipowners. Slop chests imposed additional obligations on masters and owners and were open to malpractice; guarding against such abuse through official regulation was too interventionist for many. As for allotment notes for dependants, these were rightly viewed as confusing the issue.

Thus, for much of the 1860s and 1870s there was general agreement that advance notes were an evil that should be eliminated. Most favoured governmental prohibition. But abolition was not as straightforward as might appear. The Royal Commission of 1873-1874, which concluded that "the system of advance notes is one great obstacle to the amelioration of the condition of merchant seamen" and recommended that they be declared illegal, recognised that there would be "some inconvenience from the abolition of the existing system" and that there might be "considerable opposition to the change in the ports."[34] Above all there was the view of many shipowners that notes were essential to recruitment in long-haul sail.

This impasse led to much wringing of hands but no action. This was due not only to the complexities of the issue but also to the fact that themes such as unseaworthy ships, overloading and marine insurance

---

[33]William Tulley, shipowner of Hull, quoted the case of penniless Scandinavian seamen arriving in the port seeking employment. See *BPP*, "Select Committee on the Merchant Seamen Bill," 1878 [205], XVI, qq. 2513-2516.

[34]*BPP*, "Royal Commission on Unseaworthy Ships," 1874, [1027-I], XXXIV, "Final Report," 11.

aroused even fiercer controversy.³⁵ On such topics, the interests of shipowners and reformers clashed and real passions were aroused. The concern over advance notes has to be seen against the backdrop of this greater struggle. Indeed, it was in this context that action was finally taken. The reforming campaigns of Plimsoll and Joseph Chamberlain are not our direct concern here – and have been fully recounted elsewhere – but the evidence suggests that both were increasingly frustrated by the lack of real progress at the end of the 1870s. It seems that Chamberlain felt it was time for decisive action and that when Plimsoll on 19 May 1880 announced his intention to resign, he had been promised that an act would be passed about grain cargoes. Two days later Plimsoll gained a more tangible reward when the government appointed a Select Committee on the losses of British ships. Simultaneously, Chamberlain introduced a bill to make the advance note illegal. This was duly passed and took effect from 1 August 1881.³⁶ After more than a decade positive action came in a swift and somewhat unexpected fashion. But abolition – though seemingly a milestone – did not end the matter.

Thus far, we have focused on the nature, consequences and campaign to abolish advance notes. But it is also useful to consider their role in terms of "mariners and markets." Abundant contemporary evidence suggests that notes were significant in two respects. First, they influenced the way labour was recruited by placing labour in the hands

---

[35]As Brassey (*British Seamen*, 211-212) observed, "It may be that the abuses, arising from the practice of giving advance notes, are of secondary consequence, when compared with the greater issues raised by Mr. Plimsoll. Many, who now feel a passing, though earnest, interest in our shipping legislation, have been drawn to the subject solely by the desire to lessen the loss of life at sea; and they may view with indifference any proposals for reforms, which do not directly tend to promote the security of life." One might add that according to Geoffrey Alderman, "Joseph Chamberlain's Attempted Reform of the British Mercantile Marine," *Journal of Transport History*, New series, I (1972), 171, "Plimsoll's voice had been strangely muted on the issue of their [advance notes] abolition."

[36]David Masters, *The Plimsoll Mark* (London, 1955); Geoffrey Alderman, "Samuel Plimsoll and the Shipping Interest," *Maritime History*, I (1970), 73-95; Alderman, "Joseph Chamberlain's Attempted Reform," 169-184; Williams, "State Regulation," 55-80; *BPP*, "Bill to Amend the Law relating to the Payment of Wages and Rating of Merchant Seamen," 1880 [119], CCIII; *BPP*, "Report on the Supply of British Seamen, the Number of Foreigners serving on Board British Merchant Ships, and the Reasons Given for their Employment, and on Crimping and other Matters bearing on those Subjects," 1886 [4709], LIX, 14-16.

of crimps who arranged and "cashed in" on their engagement. Second, advances were an essential element in the hiring of labour. A further, though subsidiary, issue is whether advance notes had any impact on wage levels. We will consider these matters in turn.

There is no doubt that advance notes influenced the way labour was recruited. Crimping was a complex business that exploited the accumulated earnings of seamen paid off after long voyages. Seamen in such circumstances remained vulnerable because they were not paid immediately and thus remained susceptible to inducements of lodgings and "jolly" company "on account."[37] In this sense, crimps accommodated (or preyed upon) seamen who had accumulated "past income." Nonetheless, seamen also had future income in the form of an advance note. Hence crimps, having provided seamen with value – genuine or otherwise – for past earnings, were anxious to get liabilities off their hands by procuring new engagements for them. Advances, with their heavy discounts and the opportunity to supply over-priced goods and services, were a further incentive. "Inward-bound" crimping, the opportunity to grab the accumulated earnings of seamen arriving, was clearly the most important element of the equation, but "outward-bound" aspects, through handling notes, also brought their share of income. Many deep-sea seamen were thus accommodated on arrival by crimps who acted as go-betweens for their charges' future employment. In practice, while seeking berths for seamen who had exhausted past earnings, crimps supplied labour to masters and shipowners. In this sense they became labour agents who could be contacted if men were required. As such, crimps played an important intermediary role that was intimately intertwined with the practice of advances. In this way, notes shaped the very form of recruitment, since an intermediary was in no way essential. As a Board of Trade report of 1886 observed:

> There is no need for such an agent anywhere in this country, as every seaman wanting employment can go of himself to the Mercantile Marine office, or direct to any ship in need of hands. The crimp exists...in the interests

---

[37]For a succinct account of the business of crimping, see Dixon, "The Rise and Fall," 49-67.

of himself...and the shipowner finds the services of the crimp useful.[38]

Advance notes were a more direct influence on the labour market as an inducement to recruitment. Many contemporaries even claimed they were essential to the hiring process. Seamen, it was said, regarded notes as one of the perquisites to join a long voyage and would not enlist without them. Was this the case? One of the problems of researching maritime labour is that evidence of the direct voice and feelings of seamen are not readily available. This is certainly the case here, for in the great wealth of material consulted for this paper none emanates from seamen themselves. Instead, one must infer the seamen's view from their actions. From these, it would appear that they favoured advances throughout the period. When abolition was threatened, there were demonstrations and strikes, although some observers suggested that such protests were instigated by crimping interests.[39] But whatever the strength of labour's view, shipowners invariably testified to official enquiries that seamen were committed to advances. When reading such claims, it is easy to infer that these were simply the comments of men who preferred to continue with the existing system of recruitment rather than suffer the inconvenience of change. After all, the prevailing system worked; while it was recognised to have abuses, the dissolute habits of seamen or their defrauding by crimps were not matters that caused most shipowners to sleep uneasily. Yet in this instance such cynical interpretations may be unfair because there is strong evidence that notes were an *essential* part of the market. This was especially clear in the 1880s. Despite the fact that the 1880 act abolished notes, advances continued to be made legally, since the law only prohibited any "document authorising or promising...the future payment of money on account of a seaman's wages conditionally on his going to sea...and made before those wages have been earned."[40] In other words, while the act aimed to abolish advances, it simply outlawed notes. Hence, as an 1886 report observed,

---

[38]*BPP*, "Report on the Supply of British Seamen," 1886 [4709], LIX, 9-10.

[39]Alderman, "Joseph Chamberlain's Attempted Reform," 174. The *St. Andrew's Waterside Mission Annual Report, 1880,* referred to the "strenuous opposition" of sailors; quoted in Palmer, "Seamen Ashore," note 76.

[40]43 & 44 Vict., c. 16.

owners were "free to make cash advances or to give the man a promissory note for any sum, and so long as payment of that note is not conditional on the man going to sea in the ship, it is not void under the statute."⁴¹ The law could be, and was, evaded by making advances under another guise, the so-called "bonus note." The Royal Commission on the Loss of Life at Sea of 1887 reported that:

> A system has been devised under which the seamen engage at nominal wages at 1s. per month for one or two months after the commencement of the voyage, and a note is given by the shipowner for the difference between the nominal and the real wages, which is payable a few days after the ship has sailed if the seamen has really shipped...It is doubtful whether these notes are legal. The shipowner, however, does not in practice dispute the note if the seamen performs his engagement and ships in the vessel. There is no practical distinction, therefore, between these "bonus notes" and the old advance notes.⁴²

The response to abolition thus was evasion; the practice persisted in another form. This surely says something about the nature of the market. Seamen continued to expect advances, and although shipowners could justifiably respond that advance notes were not permitted, it proved necessary to meet seamen's demands through subterfuge. As early as August 1882, Chamberlain privately admitted doubts about "the wisdom of our legislation on advance notes."⁴³ The 1887 Commission not only recognised that abolition had been "quite ineffectual" but also noted that far from improving and protecting the position of seamen, it had made them even more vulnerable since discounters of bonus notes – who were more at risk because of the dubious legal status of such instruments – demanded even greater margins than in the past. Moreover, while it had been required to enter details about the advance note on crew agree-

---

⁴¹*BPP*, "Report on the Supply of British Seamen," 1886 [4709], LIX, 14-16.

⁴²*BPP*, "Royal Commission on Loss of Life at Sea," 1887 [5227], XLIII, "Final Report," 28-29.

⁴³Quoted in Alderman, "Joseph Chamberlain's Attempted Reform," 174.

ments, no record of the new form of advances was kept.[44] The Royal Commission concluded that:

> ...the growth of this new practice shows that it is almost impossible to dispense altogether with a system, under which seamen can obtain some advance of their wages before proceeding to sea, and out of which they can procure new kits and other necessaries. We believe it will be the wisest course to recognise this necessity, and to legalise advance notes, limiting them in all cases to the amount of one month's wages.[45]

This recommendation was accepted and in 1889 advance notes for up to one month's wages were legalised. It would appear then that advance notes were essential for recruitment. Seamen expected them and, after 1881, owners felt it necessary to devise new means of paying advances.

Apart from men and masters, the further element in the labour market was the crimp who for obvious reasons wished to see the practice continue. And herein is the heart of the matter. While seamen demanded advances, were such demands irresistible? The willingness of owners to continue the practice may lie in the fact that, however much they disliked notes, they gained some benefits from the involvement of crimps who acted as labour agents but, far more crucially, could deliver. Owners and masters could hire crews in other ways, but could they ensure that the men turned up at the time of sailing? The crimp could and would do so because of his pecuniary interest.[46] The "essential" quality of advances in recruitment was perhaps more subtle than might first appear.

---

[44]*BPP*, "Report on the Supply of British Seamen," 1886 [4709], LIX, 15-16. Clauses to remedy this and to ensure the keeping of a record were included in an 1884 bill which, however, was subsequently dropped.

[45]*BPP*, "Royal Commission on Loss of Life at Sea," 1887 [5227], XLIII, 29.

[46]Before 1880, when notes had legal standing, crimps were among the most active in encouraging court action against seamen who "failed to join." They provided information and gave evidence not so much in the hope of regaining advances but rather to discourage others. For examples of such behaviour, see *BPP*, "Select Committee on the Merchant Seamen Bill," 1878 [205], XVI, qq. 165-170, 448-454, 693-704 and 1563-1581.

A final issue to consider is whether advances had any effect on wages. There were suggestions that they served as inducements and thus enabled owners to pay lower wages. Brassey believed that "with many shipowners, their attachment to the system of the advance note arises from a well-founded apprehension that some increase in the rate of wages would follow upon the abolition of advances."[47] Still, the evidence for advances affecting wages is limited. True, a Commander Bevis in 1852 supplied details of wages in Liverpool which included rates of £3 to North America with no advance or £2 10s with one month's advance, and to China of £2 5s with one month's advance or £2 with two months' advance.[48] Twenty years later, Robert Rankin, a leading figure in the North American timber trade, claimed that he hired good men without advances but had to pay fifteen shillings or £1 per month above current rates.[49] Responses to an enquiry on whether advances were accompanied by lower wages, contained in a questionnaire sent to Superintendents of twenty-nine Mercantile Marine Offices in 1886, were varied, but most reported that advances were still widely given and that wage rates were not affected other than where bonus notes led to the nominal wage of 1s for the first month.[50] Indeed, given the volume of material on advances, references to any negative effect on wages were minimal. Rankin's claims may simply reflect that an owner had to pay a considerable premium if, contrary to custom, he did not provide the perquisite, rather than any general lower wage rates associated with advances.[51] Overall, the impact of advance notes on the market lay in organisation and the strength of customary practice.

---

[47]Brassey, *British Seamen*, 180.

[48]*BPP*, "Correspondence on Manning of the Royal Navy," 1852-1853 [1628], LX.

[49]*BPP*, "Royal Commission on Unseaworthy Ships," 1873, [853], XXXVI, qq. 6756-6759.

[50]*BPP*, "Report on the Supply of British Seamen," 1886 [4709], LIX, 34-41.

[51]The emphasis here is on a "considerable premium." Contemporaries of Rankin reported that offers of an additional five or ten shillings per month without an advance had not been taken up by seamen. See *BPP*, "Royal Commission on Unseaworthy Ships," 1874, [1027-I], XXXIV, qq. 16,260-16,261; *BPP*, "Select Committee on the Merchant Seamen Bill," 1878 [205], XVI, qq. 1683-1687.

The advance note then was a form of payment peculiar to shipping in the age of sail. Its origins lay in the special needs of seamen to equip themselves for long-distance voyages. Though designed for a useful function, its operation led to abuses and from the mid-nineteenth century provoked criticism. Despite repeated demands, it was not abolished until 1880. Even then notes persisted through evasion until officially legalised in 1889. Such resilience stemmed from the role of the advance note in determining the pattern of labour supply and recruitment.

What became of the advance note after 1889? Ironically, given all the controversy engendered, the answer is not a great deal. Notes continued to be issued and the Superintendents of Mercantile Marine offices in London, Greenock, Hull and Barry testified to this in 1897. Yet the London Superintendent observed "but I may mention that now when the proportion of steamers is 537 to 87 sailing vessels, men are more continued from voyage to voyage." Likewise, the veteran campaigner for seamen's welfare, Commander Dawson, noted the decline of crimping other than in ports with a large number of long-distance sail trades.[52] The implication is that advance notes persisted but withered under competition from steam and the decline of sail within British shipping. The shift to steam, and the development of a new maritime labour market that did not feature pre-payment of wages, made notes of declining consequence. Advances soon ceased to be a concern in Britain. A Board of Trade Committee on the Manning of British Merchant Ships in 1896 ignored the subject, and an official 1897 report looked at the engagement and discharge of British seamen at continental rather than home ports.[53] By the early twentieth century the practice was effectively an anachronism. But the rapidity of its demise should not obscure its importance to the market for labour in the age of sail.

---

[52]*BPP*, "Report of the Committee to consider the Engagement and Discharge of British Seamen at Continental Ports," 1897 [8577], LXXXVIII, qq. 100-127, 140-206, 360-416, 465-473 and 2119-2121.

[53]The 1896 study is *BPP*, "Report of the Committee appointed by the Board of Trade to inquire into the Manning of British Merchant Ships," 1896 [8129], XL and XLI.

Finnish and International Maritime Labour in the Age of Sail: Was There a Market?

Yrjö Kaukiainen

The existence of a competitive, efficient and virtually global freight market in the late nineteenth century is indisputable. At the same time, because fleets like the British and American employed many foreign seamen, it seems possible that there even was a parallel market for maritime labour.[1] Recently, however, Charles P. Kindleberger expressed strong doubts about the existence of *efficient* maritime labour markets.[2] His arguments were primarily provoked by some sweeping statements in a collection edited by David W. Galenson;[3] perhaps for this reason his book is more a commentary than a monograph. Yet his main points merit consideration. He argues that labour markets were not efficient because the violence and force exerted to enlist and supervise sailors meant that they were not voluntary participants. Moreover, he stresses that because wages differed among various fleets there was little market integration, a feature repeatedly argued by Lewis R. Fischer.[4]

---

[1]Rosemary E. Ommer, "'Composed of All Nationalities': The Crews of Windsor Vessels," in R. Ommer and G. Panting (eds.), *Working Men Who Got Wet* (St. John's, 1980), 191-227; Lewis R. Fischer and Helge W. Nordvik, "Finländare i den kanadensiska handelsflottan 1863-1913," *Historisk Tidskrift för Finland*, LXXIII, No. 3 (1988), 373-394.

[2]Charles P. Kindleberger, *Mariners and Markets* (New York, 1992).

[3]David W. Galenson (ed.), *Markets in History: Economic Studies of the Past* (Cambridge, 1989).

[4]See, for example, Lewis R. Fischer, "Seamen in a Space Economy: International Regional Patterns of Maritime Wages on Sailing Vessels," in S. Fisher (ed.), *Lisbon as a Port Town, the British Seamen and Other Maritime Themes* (Exeter, 1988), 57-92; and Fischer, "Around the Rim: Seamen's Wages in North Sea Ports, 1863-1900," in L.R.

Still, I cannot escape the feeling that the historical development of labour markets, whether national or international, is difficult to comprehend in purely neo-classical terms. Microeconomic theory views labour markets as similar to commodity markets: labour is supposedly an uniform "commodity" which can be bought and sold, with its price depending on supply and demand. But this often does not conform with the real world.[5] In the modern world, for example, trade unions and other organizations affect the market decisively. Indeed, even during the nineteenth century – when unions were rare and political economy was often based on the principle of *laissez-faire* – labour was subjected to important spatial and social constraints. The most fundamental difference from commodity markets is the fact that labour markets involve human beings who could not be transported like logs and had social ties and preferences of their own. While the nineteenth-century European grain market could be affected by knowledge of the last rice harvest in Burma – since rice could be transported from the other side of the globe in a matter of months – the existence of a large unemployed pool of labour in eastern Europe had no direct bearing on North American wages because the Polish or Russian rural proletariat could not be employed on the other side of the Atlantic. Of course, seasonal labour migrations over relatively long distances have occurred for many years but, in addition to being costly, have been limited by various societal and governmental barriers. In principle, the labour force consisted of people residing in local communities. The seamen who manned foreign vessels far from home were in fact exceptional. While the internationality of maritime labour markets makes them unusually interesting, when discussing Kindleberger's theses the local markets remain of primary importance. In the following essay I will therefore first look at them and only later discuss the degree of integration.

In Finland, as well as in Sweden, the maritime labour market was controlled by public institutions, *sjömanshus* (literally "seamen's houses"), which were in many respects comparable with the British

---

Fischer, *et al.* (eds.), *The North Sea. Twelve Essays on Social History of Maritime Labour* (Stavanger, 1992), 59-73.

[5]Even Kindleberger, *Mariners*, xv, refers briefly to another tradition – represented, for example, by Karl Polanyi and Robert Solow – which regards labour markets differently than commodity markets; for some reason, however, he does not discuss the issue.

Mercantile Marine offices. The system was founded in the mid-eighteenth century to register sailors and to make it easier for the navy to enrol more men in wartime. Accordingly, it aimed to control the labour market in mercantilist sense rather than to create an efficient forum for hiring seamen. In practice, however, military requirements gave way to market exigencies: the *sjömanshus* developed into an institution which enabled supply and demand to find an equilibrium in a practical and relatively free manner.

In the late nineteenth century, every major seaport in Finland had a *sjömanshus*, and every Finnish sailor going abroad was supposed to be enrolled in one. This took place automatically when a man was hired for the first time; although a small fee was charged and an oath of loyalty administered, no system to reject prospective seamen was devised. A master or shipowner could hire men as they saw fit, but each agreement was controlled and registered by the local *sjömanshus*. In practice, even hiring normally was carried out at the "house." In most towns this took place on Sunday. If a ship needed crew, the flag of the *sjömanshus* was hoisted so that everyone looking for work would know. Men gathering outside were then told what jobs were available and each candidate was led inside to negotiate his position and wage with the shipowner in question. While it may be thought that the bargaining position of a sailor in such circumstances was poor, at least experienced men were able to see the relationship between applicants and positions and to adjust their wage demands accordingly.[6]

"Non-market" factors may also have affected wage bargaining. Married men traditionally were paid more than bachelors, while accepted wage norms or ideas about "just pay" may have reduced wage fluctuations. It is also possible that local shipowners cooperated to keep wages down, but this became increasingly difficult as demand grew. Moreover, even if a sailor were compelled to accept a wage he later regarded as too low, he had an opportunity to remedy this by deserting.

---

[6]There are many published reminiscences and detailed descriptions about the hiring of seamen. See, for example, Samuli Paulaharju, *Vanha Raahe* (Porvoo, 1925), 256-258; Lauri Pyy, "Merimieselämää Raahessa ja raahelaisella laivalla vv. 1855-75," *Kyläkirjaston Kuvalehti*, A-series, no. 7-8 (1914). There are also several archives of local *sjömanshus* still in existence (e.g., Helsinki, Turku, Rauma and Oulu) and the working of the system can be followed through their rolls and lists of recruited and discharged sailors.

Another feature which complicated the impact of supply and demand on wages was job stratification based on skills and experience. In Finland, as in other Nordic countries, there were no less than four different ranks "before the mast," in addition to boys. The two lowest, *jungman* and *lättmatros*, normally equated with British ordinary seamen (OSs), although some *jungmen* were in fact boys. The *matros* was synonymous with able-bodied seamen (ABs), and there were also bosuns and carpenters. While wages were roughly comparable within ranks there were no uniform definitions; even this could be a matter for negotiation. Thus, both wages and ranks could vary according to local traditions and individual agreements; wages within a single rank did not necessarily provide an accurate picture of overall wage levels in different ports.

The differentiation of ranks may also have increased wage inelasticity. When the demand for sailors increased, more inexperienced hands were typically hired. But since neophytes were paid less than experienced sailors the general level of wages, or the wages paid in the lower ranks, did not increase along correspondingly. In Finland, however, wage changes did correlate roughly with demand. During the 1860s and early 1870s, when most local merchant tonnage increased, the general level of wages – and of ABs in particular – rose, while the opposite happened during the great depression of the 1880s.[7]

On the other hand, it is clear that the level of wages was not the only or most important inducement to a career at sea. Many boys enlisted because of romantic ideas or "to see the world;" such recruits were obviously willing to accept low stipends. The great breach between image and reality resulted in a substantial proportion of beginners deciding never to return to sea, but even short-term sailors were part of the labour force. Moreover, this was an occupation for the young; few were willing or able to combine marriage and seafaring.

Nineteenth-century Finnish local markets for maritime labour may not have been perfect in the neo-classical sense – wages were somewhat inelastic and they were affected by non-economic factors. But it is clear that the system was voluntary: there was no coercion in hiring. If men felt compelled to go to sea this was only for economic reasons, and if many boys went to sea because of unrealistic ideas it was their own choice. If these local markets were not efficient by present standards

---

[7]Yrjö Kaukiainen, *Sailing into Twilight: Finnish Shipping in an Age of Transport Revolution, 1860-1914* (Jyväskylä, 1991), 111-116.

they at least worked. Indeed, it may be difficult to find better nineteenth-century labour markets.

While observations about a peripheral country cannot always be applied to the big maritime nations, if a minor nation had a functioning labour market can we imagine the core lacking one? Certainly British shipping offices seem to have functioned efficiently as local labour markets. Even in distant Calcutta, if we are to believe Rudyard Kipling, sailors used to come to the local shipping office in search of a new berth, as did masters looking for men.[8] It is illustrative that Finnish masters who had lost men were able to find replacements (even Scandinavians, whom they preferred) in London, Liverpool, Cardiff, Pensacola, Hong Kong and elsewhere, if they were willing to pay prevailing local wages.

Kindleberger makes a great issue of crimps and shanghaiing. Indeed, he claims that crimping was "the merchant-marine counterpart of the press-gang."[9] It is true that crimps were regarded as evil; Britain, for example, agreed to try to prevent crimps from helping men desert from Russian and Finnish ships.[10] But such a concern reflects shipowners' rather than seamen's views. Desertion was a grave problem for the former simply because masters often had to hire new men at much higher wages than the deserters commanded. For sailors, on the other hand, jumping a ship may be regarded as a rational means of improving wages or even protesting against bad food or harsh discipline. In these cases, boardinghouse keepers and crimps, as shady as many were, could be regarded as middlemen who helped rather than hindered market forces.

So far, I have not seen any attempts to estimate the significance of crimping to the recruitment of seamen. It is true that desertion was common in the 1860s, 1870s, 1880s and 1890s. In two Atlantic Canadian fleets, twenty-two to twenty-three percent of men serving on sailing vessels between 1863 and 1913 deserted, and Finnish figures from the

---

[8]Rudyard Kipling, "City of Dreadful Night," *From Sea to Sea: Letters of Travel* (2 vols., Garden City, NY, 1907), II, 233-234.

[9]Kindleberger, *Mariners*, 20.

[10]See, for example, Kustaa Hautala, "Merimiesten karkaaminen suomalaisilta laivoilta," in *Näkökulmia menneisyyteen. Eino Jutikkalan juhlakirja* (Porvoo, 1967).

1860s and 1870s suggest similar proportions.[11] It would, however, be bold to assume that all were persuaded or aided by a crimp – on the contrary, there must have been many who did it on their own initiative or were coaxed by a shipmate. Crimps may have been invaluable in some circumstances: since a deserter did not dare go to a shipping office as long as his original ship was in port, an underground middleman was perhaps the only route to rapid employment. No doubt many poor sailors were cheated by crimps and "sold" to ships against their will, but the presence of swindling is no direct measure of market inefficiency. Moreover, I am inclined to accept the view presented by Lewis R. Fischer, who claimed that many deserters were "very much in control of their own destinies" and desertion was often a rational choice.[12]

Brutal discipline was another factor, according to Kindleberger, characteristic of an inefficient market. In principle, this is important because it is intuitively plausible that efficiency was more likely a function of economic rewards than of coercion or brutality. Yet disciplinary norms, like wages, probably depended in the long run more on cultural traditions than economic rationality. Discipline was also fairly strict in manufacturing and public works.[13] That it obviously was tougher on deep-sea ships is not too difficult to fathom: masters had to compel seamen to do things they did not like, such as reefing a sail in the middle of a storm or unloading coal in the tropics. Detachment from land-based authorities further increased the need for strong measures. While brutal discipline was a dangerous antidote – if administered too liberally it could diminish the labour supply and increase desertions – it is too dogmatic to deny a market's existence because of brutality. For example, the brutality of war did not prevent the formation of a market for mercenaries in early modern Europe.

---

[11]Lewis R. Fischer, "A Dereliction of Duty: The Problem of Desertion on Nineteenth Century Sailing Vessels," in Ommer and Panting (eds.), *Working Men*, 54-57; Yrjö Kaukiainen, "Five Years Before the Mast: Observations on the Conditions of Maritime Labour in Finland and Elsewhere," *Research in Maritime History*, No. 3 (December 1992), 51.

[12]Fischer, "Dereliction," 54.

[13]For a recent discussion on industrial discipline, see James S. Roberts, "Drink and Industrial Discipline in Nineteenth-Century Germany," in L.R. Berlanstein (ed.), *The Industrial Revolution and Work in Nineteenth-Century Europe* (London, 1992), 102-124.

In summary, I believe that there were functioning *local* markets for sailors, not only in Sweden and Finland but in many maritime nations. Although wages could be somewhat inelastic and the actual control of work relied more on force than on economic rewards, supply and demand were able to intersect and, most important, this occurred not because of coercion but due to factors which were genuinely economic. Nonetheless, at least in Finland, these markets were local rather than national. Even in the 1860s and 1870s, most seamen in the smaller Finnish coastal towns were from the town or its vicinity.[14] Still, it would be an exaggeration to claim that they were only local: many men, particularly masters and mates, sailed on ships from towns more distant. Moreover, although there were substantial local differences, there was indeed something which could be called a national level of wages.[15]

The next question is whether these local markets were integrated to any significant degree? As mentioned before, Kindleberger firmly claims that this was not the case. His conclusions were based, above all, on the material presented by Lewis R. Fischer and some of his colleagues which do amply demonstrate two important things. First, wage differences between ports, not only across the Atlantic and around the North Sea but even in Norway, were sufficiently substantial that it is difficult to think of a single integrated market. This is corroborated by the observation that wages in different ports did not fluctuate similarly. Thus, the markets were not integrated, at least in the conventional sense.

But all the comparisons known to me have been based on nominal wages and the various currencies have been compared by relying on common exchange rates. Real wages – the actual buying power of local wages, as measured for example by the purchasing power parities used by Angus Maddison in his international comparisons of economic growth – could differ from such values. It is at least a realistic assump-

---

[14]Jari Lybeck, "Sjöfolket i Raumo under sjöfartens expansionsår 1840-1870," *Historisk Tidskrift för Finland*, LXXIII, No. 3 (1988), 542. I have made similar observations for Oulu and Hannu Kujala has presented comparative material from Turku in an unpublished manuscript he has kindly lent me. Helsinki was an exception (Christian Ahlström, "Sjömän i Helsingfors 1819-1849," *Historisk Tidskrift för Finland*, LXXIII, No. 3 [1988], 515), but this is not surprising because there was substantial immigration.

[15]See Kaukiainen, *Sailing into Twilight*, 111-113. The same applies to the wages of casual landward labour; see, for example, Heimer Björkqvist, *Prisrörelser och penningvärde i Finland under guldmyntfotsperioden* (Helsingfors, 1958), 344.

tion that the price levels of necessities was lower in the periphery and higher in the big metropolises. If sailors had been paid a regular monthly wage in varying currencies this would, of course, be no major issue but, in reality, most received the best part of their pay only when the ship returned home. Moreover, a third or half of the wages of married men had already been paid to their wives. This means that the actual income of seamen compared mainly with living costs at home. It would be quite daring to suppose that a common seamen commanded such a knowledge of exchange rates that he would have been able accurately to compare wages in different currencies – at least in this respect the neo-classical assumption of perfect knowledge does not seem fully realistic.

Moreover, as I pointed out earlier, there are important differences between commodity and labour markets. It is difficult to create a large labour market with equal and highly-correlated wages. Supposing that wage differences reflect, however roughly, variations between supply and demand, this would require the elimination of such variances by moving people from "surplus" to "deficit" areas. Because labour was not as mobile as products, this would require a structural change and an acceptance that equilibrium could not be reached in the short term.

Another possible condition (at least in theory) for achieving an integrated international maritime labour market would require the separation of "seaward" from "landward" labour markets. This, in fact, is a common hypothesis, which even Kindleberger seems to accept.[16] It is true that in most Finnish ports sailors and "landward" labourers formed two antagonistic, almost hostile, groups and there even seem to have been distinctions between coastal and deep-sea sailors.[17] A closer inspection, though, reveals that the "seaward" and "landward" labour markets were connected. Although there were many jobs at sea that required special skills and experience, there were others which necessitated only muscle power. All sailors were not necessarily skilled workers and a good number of inexperienced hands could be (and were) shipped to complete the crew. The large proportion of short-term, "one-voyage," sailors as well as the normal drop-out of older men, required a fairly steady influx of new labour from local "landward" sources. Thus, anyone physically capable could become a sailor; the maritime labour market

---

[16]Kindleberger, *Mariners*, xvi.

[17]See Paulaharju, *Vanha Raahe*.

was totally open at the "bottom" end. Moreover, even most long-term sailors returned to "landward" work in their late thirties. All this means that seamen's wages could never be fully detached from local remuneration for casual workers. If sailors in far-away Oulu (Uleåborg) had demanded wages similar to those paid in London or New York, shipowners would have found beginners (and even experienced sailors) willing to work for lower pay. A substantial rise in seamen's wages would have required comparative increases in "landward" pay as well.

Such a conclusion, however, does not render international wage differentials irrelevant. Indirectly they could certainly affect the labour market in low-wage countries. There was an opportunity cost which a Finnish sailor on a domestic vessel faced: the higher wage he could receive abroad *minus* travelling and other expenses (a good example of "transaction costs") incurred in journeying to a high-wage port. As long as this did not exceed domestic wages, the latter were not affected; in fact, it may be assumed that even a modest excess remained unnoticed in a peripheral region because of practical difficulties in communication and because men were unaccustomed to travel at their own expense.[18] A far more practical plan was to take a job aboard a domestic ship and desert abroad. Thus, the wage difference may have affected Finnish wages mainly by increasing desertion to an unacceptable level. Yet it is unclear whether shipowners identified such a relationship at all.

On a practical level, foreign wages also directly affected Finnish ships: when men were hired in foreign, high-wage ports, even Finnish-born seamen received better pay than those engaged in Finland. Accordingly, the actual wage costs were higher than would have been predicted from the initial payroll. On the other hand, men hired in Finland who remained on board seldom managed to get any raise at all. Indeed, it was typical that their wages remained markedly lower than those of their fellow countrymen hired abroad. Such inflexibility was possible simply because most of the wages were paid only at the end of the voyage.

Wage signals may have been weak, but if we look at the actual movement of workers there was an international labour market. "High-demand" areas, like North America and Britain, received sailors from the low-wage rim. For example, in 1881 the number of Finnish sailors on foreign vessels was estimated at 6000, a number which roughly equalled

---

[18]Such travelling became more common only during the 1880s when the domestic demand for maritime labour declined. See Hautala, "Merimiesten," 115.

those manning Finnish deep-sea vessels. Moreover, the core of these itinerant sailors remained abroad permanently. A sample of Canadian fleets in the years 1863 to 1913 contained about 5600 Finnish sailors, the majority of whom had served on foreign vessels before signing-on to a Canadian ship.[19] These men had paid their "transaction" costs and in the process had exiled themselves from their country and local pools of labour. Many perhaps were "scallywags," misfits did not wish to return to normal "landward" society.[20] Yet they sailed in the same vessels and received wages similar to those paid their less adventurous colleagues. They did not really comprise a separate or detached labour market.

It therefore seems that there was in the latter half of the nineteenth century a network of more or less connected local maritime labour markets which made it possible for sailors to find jobs on vessels of different nations. The wages were not uniform nor necessarily tending in that direction, but they were nonetheless connected by supply and demand. This was certainly not the neoclassicist's ideal market; whether it was efficient depends on how the term is defined. Instead of referring to theoretical definitions it might be more useful to ask how well the system worked in mediating demand and supply. In response, it may be noted that a fairly large and representative Finnish data set did not contain a single case in which a ship was deprived of its intended deployment because of a lack of crew.[21] On the other hand, during depressions it was common for vessels to be laid-up because no profitable freight was available. Still, it would be difficult to claim that the international freight market was not efficient.

It is significant that after the First World War the maritime labour market actually became less "international." In many countries seamen's unions adopted policies that made it more difficult for foreigners to be engaged. Accordingly, the markets for mariners became more "nationalized" than they were in the age of sail.

---

[19]Yrjö Kaukiainen, "Från jungman Jansson till Kalle Aaltonen," *Historisk Tidskrift för Finland*, LXXIII, No. 3 (1988), 363; Fischer and Nordvik, "Finländare," 377-383.

[20]Rudyard Kipling, "City," II, 235, described such men in Calcutta: "They sail the sea because they must live; and there is no end to their toil. Very, very few find haven of any kind, and the earth, whose ways they do not understand, is cruel to them, when they walk upon it to drink and be merry after the manner of beasts."

[21]Kaukiainen, *Sailing into Twilight*, 221-229.

The Efficiency of Maritime Labour Markets in the Age of Sail: The Post-1850 Norwegian Experience[1]

Lewis R. Fischer

Introduction

By the mid-nineteenth century most seamen who manned the world's merchant marines were recruited on exchanges which at least superficially resembled markets, places where buyers (masters) and sellers (seamen) of maritime labour reached agreement on conditions of employment.[2] There is nothing startling about this; at least in the western world, most labour was hired in this way. Yet we know little about how the process worked – or works. Indeed, notwithstanding its admitted importance, labour economics remains one of the least developed sub-disciplines of the broader profession. But if these generalizations are broadly true – as I believe them to be – there are signs that things are changing. The publication in 1989 of the essays that comprise *Markets in History* was a major watershed.[3] In maritime history, it can be argued that the appearance three years later of Charles P. Kindleberger's idiosyncratic

---

[1]While this essay uses insights from several projects undertaken over the past two decades, most of the data come from a project on Norwegian wages. I would like to thank Helge W. Nordvik, my co-investigator on this project, for his assistance with the data collection and much more. My work on maritime wages has been generously financed principally by the Social Sciences and Humanities Research Council of Canada, to which I extend my gratitude.

[2]For a discussion of how markets for merchant seamen worked, see Lewis R. Fischer, "International Maritime Labour, 1863-1900: Wages and Trends," *The Great Circle*, X, No. 1 (1988), 1-21.

[3]David W. Galenson (ed.), *Markets in History: Economic Studies of the Past* (Cambridge, 1989). Of particular interest to maritime historians in this volume will be Lance E. Davis, Robert E. Gallman and Teresa D. Hutchins, "Productivity in American Whaling: The New Bedford Fleet in the Nineteenth Century," which is found on 97-147.

Mariners and Markets served a similar function.⁴ There can be little doubt that maritime historians needed prodding. Indeed, one of the defining characteristics of maritime economic history has been that even studies which clearly focus on labour have tended to be relatively unconcerned about markets.⁵

Economists have typically treated labour, along with land and capital, as one of the three standard factors of production. As a result, it has long been generally accepted that a rational treatment of labour was fundamental both to theory and to an understanding of the way an economy functions. Yet most economists would agree that not all labour issues properly belong to the sphere of economics. Indeed, most labour economists have largely (but not exclusively) concentrated on the allocation function. In so doing neo-classicists have tended to make four assumptions: 1) that labour markets are recognizably free; 2) that individuals offer well-defined labour services; 3) that the labour offered is voluntary; and 4) that at some point labour markets will clear, whatever that means.⁶

This is not the place for a full-blown critique of neo-classical assumptions. But it is important to recognize that it is virtually impossible to operationalize many of these assumptions clearly and discretely and hence to test their validity. More apposite to this particular study is the fact that these assumptions do not really help to get at the question upon which I want to focus: if labour markets existed in the period 1850-

---

⁴Charles P. Kindleberger, *Mariners and Markets* (New York, 1992). In characterizing Kindleberger's volume as "idiosyncratic," I mean to convey the idea, which I have no doubt he would accept, that it is less a thorough treatment of maritime labour markets than an extended suggestive essay designed to fuel debate and to stimulate research.

⁵This is meant not as a criticism but as an observation, for there are a host of legitimate questions that need to be posed. For some examples of various questions about labour asked recently by maritime historians, see Eric W. Sager, *Seafaring Labour: The Merchant Marine of Atlantic Canada, 1820-1914* (Montréal, 1989); Marcus Rediker, *Between the Devil and the Deep Blue Sea: Merchant Seamen, Pirates and the Anglo-American Maritime World* (Cambridge, 1987); Judith Fingard, *Jack in Port: Sailortowns of Eastern Canada* (Toronto, 1982); and Valerie C. Burton, "Apprenticeship Regulation and Maritime Labour in the Nineteenth-Century British Merchant Marine," *International Journal of Maritime History*, I, No. 1 (1989), 29-49.

⁶R. Tarling, "Labour Markets," in John Eatwell, *et al.* (eds.), *The New Palgrave: A Dictionary of Economics* (4 vols., London, 1987), III, 86-88.

1914, were they also efficient? To try to shed some light on this problem, I have decided here to focus on a single country, Norway. In making this choice, I can hardly be accused of selecting an insignificant maritime nation. In the sixty-five years between the repeal of the British Navigation Acts and the outbreak of the First World War the Norwegian merchant marine expanded from less than 300,000 gross registered tons (grt) to a carrying capacity of well over 1,700,000 grt. By 1875 Norwegians owned the third largest fleet in the world, a relative position they more-or-less retained for the next forty years. Indeed, investment in the merchant marine was so dynamic in this era that it served as an "engine of economic growth" for the national economy, generating a disproportionate share of both employment and income, especially in the years before 1880 and again from the late 1890s to 1914.[7]

More important, I have also decided to use Charles Kindleberger's own criteria to see how efficient maritime labour markets were. He suggests four primary gauges of efficiency: 1) the degree of freedom (as opposed to coercion) that characterizes labour's decision to participate in the exchange; 2) the extent of "wage equalization;" 3) how well markets equalize supply and demand; and 4) the amount of stability of employment. The analysis to follow suggests strongly that while there were indeed local markets by 1914, they were still, in Kindleberger's terms, relatively inefficient. The measure of this inefficiency is that only the first criterion was achieved unambiguously by the outbreak of World War I. The last three factors present more problems. For this reason, I intend to focus in this essay predominantly on the last three, and especially on the question of wage equalization, which I believe to be the most important indicator of market efficiency.[8]

---

[7]For an overview of the development of the Norwegian shipping industry in this period, see Helge W. Nordvik, "The Shipping Industries of the Scandinavian Countries, 1850-1914," in Lewis R. Fischer and Gerald E. Panting (eds.), *Change and Adaptation in Maritime History: The North Atlantic Fleets in the Nineteenth Century* (St. John's, 1985), 117-148. The Norwegian experience is placed in international perspective in Lewis R. Fischer and Helge W. Nordvik, "Maritime Transport and the Integration of the North Atlantic Economy, 1850-1914," in Wolfram Fischer, R. Marvin McInnis and Jürgen Schneider (eds.), *The Emergence of a World Economy, 1500-1914* (Wiesbaden, 1986), 519-544.

[8]Equalization is also, it must be admitted, the easiest of these factors to test empirically.

Free Will

It is clear that virtually all participants in the Norwegian maritime labour market between 1850 and 1914 were there of their own volition. While the tremendous expansion in the maritime world – and in the international economy generally – between 1850 and 1914 meant that there were often disjunctions between supply and demand, equilibrium was achieved in most ports in reasonably good order. Indeed, especially in Europe, wage stability was arguably the most obvious characteristic of maritime labour markets after 1850. This is not to deny, however, that some labour was forcibly enlisted. If the world's merchant navies for the most part were not the result of press gangs, there were other ways of compelling individuals to serve. In western ports the most important mechanism was the use of crimps.[9]

While it would be foolish to deny that crimps existed or that they did not play an important role in many local and regional maritime labour markets, they do not appear to have been a problem in Norway. None of the standard histories of Norwegian ports has found crimping to be widespread or terribly significant in recruiting labour, and I have found no evidence in previous market studies of anomalies that might suggest a major crimping presence.[10]

Still, this is not to argue that all Norwegians who served at sea were necessarily enthusiastic about doing so. Some (it is impossible to be precise about the numbers) were likely forced by poverty or the lack of alternative employment opportunities to enlist. One reflection of this, of course, was the fact that nineteenth-century Norway contributed a higher proportion of its population to transatlantic migrations than any other European land and that some of this was doubtless due to "push" factors.[11] But without trivializing this point, it is important to note that

---

[9]The best study of crimping remains Fingard, *Jack in Port*.

[10]See, for example, Lauritz Pettersen. *Bergen og sjøfarten. III: Fra kjøpmannsrederi til selvstendig næring 1860-1914* (Bergen, 1984). In the Nordic countries the only one in which crimping was likely an important means of providing labour was Denmark, and especially the city of Copenhagen.

[11]For a study of this flow with a maritime emphasis, see Lewis R. Fischer, "The Sea as Highway: Maritime Service as a Means of International Migration, 1863-1913," in Klaus Friedland (ed.), *Maritime Aspects of Migration* (Köln, 1990), 293-307.

this is a different kind of compulsion than Kindleberger discussed. It would seem that by the first criteria Norwegian maritime labour markets may have been fairly efficient in the last half of the nineteenth century.

Wage Equalization

If Norwegians who went to sea appear to have done so more or less of their own free will, an examination of wage equalization does not lend solid support to any argument that wages in the various Norwegian ports were becoming more equal. To see whether there is evidence of spatial market integration, I want to use some evidence from an earlier research project on Norwegian wages. The sources, which have been described elsewhere, enable an examination of both sail and steam wages.[12] But to conserve space, I will confine the analysis in this section to sailing vessels (steam will be added to the mix in the next section of the paper).

It would be possible to analyze twenty-three Norwegian ports during the period under consideration, but to present data for all would consume far too much space. Instead, I have selected four ports for more intensive investigation, each of which is broadly representative of a specific region of the country. From Oslofjørd in the southeast, I have selected the port of Tønsberg, a major shipping town which I know from other work had wages generally typical of those elsewhere in the region. From the south coast I have chosen Risør, one of the major ports for sailing vessels and the home of a variety of types of shipowners, both large and small. From the west coast I have picked Trondheim, an industrial town with a fair-sized fleet. Finally, I have also selected from the west coast the town of Kristiansund, which was among other things a major fishing port and hence had an alternative source of maritime employment. It is well to admit, however, that in choosing the ports to examine in this paper, I have been concerned not simply with their representativeness but also with whether or not I have fairly continuous time series. For this reason, some fairly obvious ports (Kristiania, Bergen, and Stavanger, for example) have been excluded.

---

[12]The most convenient source is probably Lewis R. Fischer and Helge W. Nordvik, "From Namsos to Halden: Myths and Realities in the History of Norwegian Seamen's Wages, 1850-1914," *Scandinavian Economic History Review*, XXXV, No. 1 (1987), 41-65.

Similarly, I have decided to focus upon specific occupations rather than analyzing all twenty-six separate occupations for which data has been collected. In this section, I want to focus on only four which are broadly representative of the various occupations that characterized shipboard organization. To examine the officer corps, I have chosen first mates; to look at skilled labour I have selected carpenters; and to examine entry level positions, I have chosen ordinary seamen. I also include cooks, largely because they are so different in Norway.[13] I exclude perhaps the most obvious choice – able-bodied seamen – since my colleague Helge Nordvik and I have written extensively about them elsewhere.[14] I will, however, bring in observations about this important class of labour at various times in the analysis.

We can begin by examining wage levels. To conserve space I do not here present the nominal wages, which are available elsewhere.[15] Instead, I present some time series which are derived from the nominal data but are more directly relevant to the question of wage differentials. Tables 1-4 depict for each of the occupations and ports the yearly mean wages expressed as indices with the national mean wages in each given year equal to one hundred. This is a quick way of seeing whether there were consistent regional differentials. Taken as a body the tables indicate that while there were no shortage of differentials, they were hardly consistent.

---

[13]For a discussion of the ways in which cooks were quantitatively different in the Norwegian merchant marine, see Lewis R. Fischer and Helge W. Nordvik, "Fish and Ships: The Social Structure of the Maritime Labour Force in Haugesund, Norway in the 1870s," *Sjøfartshistorisk Årbok 1986* (Bergen, 1987), 139-170; Lewis R. Fischer, "The Price of Labour: Seamen's Wages in the British, Canadian and Norwegian Merchant Marines, 1863-1913," in Lewis R. Fischer and Helge W. Nordvik (eds.), *Across the Broad Atlantic: Essays in Comparative Canadian-Norwegian Maritime History, 1850-1914* (St. John's, 1995), forthcoming.

[14]See Lewis R. Fischer and Helge W. Nordvik, "Norwegian Matroser: Seafarers and National Labour Markets in Norway, 1850-1914," *Scandinavian-Canadian Studies*, IV (1989), 58-81; Fischer and Nordvik, "Wages in the Norwegian Maritime Sector, 1850-1914: A Re-Interpretation," in Lewis R. Fischer, Helge W. Nordvik and Walter E. Minchinton (eds.), *Shipping and Trade in the Northern Seas, 1600-1939* (Bergen, 1988), 14-35; Fischer and Nordvik, "From Namsos to Halden," 55-57.

[15]See Lewis R. Fischer and Helge W. Nordvik, "The Regional Economy of Late Nineteenth Century Norway: Maritime Wages as a Measure of Spatial Inequality, 1850-1914," in Illka Nummela (ed.), *Sitä Kuusta Kuuleninen* (Jyväskylä, 1989), 89-112.

Table 1
First Mates' Wages Compared to National Means, Selected Ports, Foreign-Going Sail, 1850-1914
(National Mean for First Mates = 100 in each year)

Year	Tø	K	Tr	R	Year	Tø	K	Tr	R
1850	102	N/A	97	N/A	1883	97	95	103	N/A
1851	100	N/A	94	N/A	1884	98	100	N/A	N/A
1852	103	N/A	95	N/A	1885	98	101	110	98
1853	103	N/A	90	N/A	1886	96	N/A	111	N/A
1854	103	N/A	93	N/A	1887	97	N/A	114	N/A
1855	103	N/A	101	N/A	1888	97	102	N/A	97
1856	N/A	N/A	102	N/A	1889	105	100	103	97
1857	109	N/A	95	N/A	1890	106	N/A	101	95
1858	100	N/A	96	N/A	1891	103	95	98	96
1859	104	N/A	101	N/A	1892	103	93	86	99
1860	104	N/A	98	N/A	1893	103	107	97	100
1861	96	N/A	103	N/A	1894	103	N/A	103	99
1862	101	N/A	99	N/A	1895	102	103	106	100
1863	101	N/A	102	N/A	1896	101	N/A	103	97
1864	108	N/A	100	102	1897	105	92	N/A	96
1865	102	N/A	95	99	1898	106	N/A	N/A	97
1866	95	N/A	95	95	1899	102	N/A	N/A	94
1867	98	95	95	97	1900	103	N/A	N/A	94
1868	98	94	100	95	1901	N/A	N/A	N/A	96
1869	96	95	N/A	97	1902	103	N/A	N/A	97
1870	94	97	99	N/A	1903	102	N/A	97	97
1871	94	93	N/A	N/A	1904	103	N/A	N/A	95
1872	100	N/A	95	N/A	1905	102	N/A	N/A	97
1873	101	N/A	91	N/A	1906	100	N/A	102	96
1874	98	N/A	95	N/A	1907	103	N/A	90	93
1875	100	N/A	89	N/A	1908	103	N/A	95	98
1876	100	94	95	N/A	1909	100	N/A	114	104
1877	97	96	95	99	1910	107	N/A	108	99
1878	96	96	102	99	1911	112	N/A	102	102
1879	93	100	113	101	1912	103	N/A	88	104
1880	96	N/A	97	99	1913	102	N/A	86	101
1881	96	N/A	90	97	1914	98	N/A	84	98
1882	92	102	95	98					

Notes: Tø = Tønsberg; K = Kristiansund; Tr = Trondheim; and R = Risør. N/A indicates no data, an insufficient number of cases for the mean to be significant, or an unacceptably high standard deviation around the mean. Prior to 1877, wages were paid in *specialdaler*; I have converted this to *kroner* at the rate of 1 *specialdaler* = 4 *kroner*.

Source: Derived from Norwegian School of Economics and Business Administration (NHH), Wedervang Archive, WA 44.

Table 2
Carpenters' Wages Compared to National Means, Selected Ports, Foreign-Going Sail, 1850-1914
(National Mean for Carpenters = 100 in each year)

Year	Tø	K	Tr	R	Year	Tø	K	Tr	R
1850	98	101	104	N/A	1883	99	96	91	N/A
1851	99	104	103	N/A	1884	101	99	N/A	N/A
1852	102	101	97	N/A	1885	100	111	89	102
1853	102	100	95	N/A	1886	101	N/A	103	N/A
1854	104	86	99	N/A	1887	101	93	104	N/A
1855	104	98	96	N/A	1888	102	99	80	98
1856	108	98	90	N/A	1889	107	95	93	95
1857	107	94	91	N/A	1890	107	87	N/A	95
1858	99	101	104	N/A	1891	106	95	N/A	94
1859	101	98	102	N/A	1892	105	95	83	99
1860	99	95	105	N/A	1893	106	90	102	96
1861	100	92	107	N/A	1894	108	91	92	100
1862	99	94	107	107	1895	109	89	94	103
1863	97	101	107	109	1896	107	83	N/A	101
1864	101	96	99	104	1897	110	N/A	N/A	98
1865	101	95	95	110	1898	109	N/A	N/A	95
1866	101	99	95	102	1899	109	N/A	N/A	95
1867	99	105	102	99	1900	106	N/A	N/A	94
1868	100	104	102	N/A	1901	N/A	N/A	N/A	97
1869	99	104	95	N/A	1902	110	N/A	N/A	91
1870	97	110	96	N/A	1903	109	N/A	92	96
1871	98	106	96	N/A	1904	108	N/A	N/A	96
1872	99	108	99	N/A	1905	104	N/A	N/A	98
1873	101	N/A	99	N/A	1906	107	103	N/A	94
1874	103	N/A	102	N/A	1907	101	97	108	93
1875	99	100	106	N/A	1908	105	N/A	95	90
1876	100	109	97	N/A	1909	104	N/A	N/A	86
1877	99	109	95	98	1910	118	N/A	N/A	102
1878	99	98	98	99	1911	116	N/A	N/A	88
1879	98	112	106	103	1912	109	N/A	N/A	81
1880	97	108	95	103	1913	111	N/A	N/A	111
1881	98	109	97	101	1914	N/A	N/A	N/A	105
1882	100	97	94	102					

Notes: See table 1.

Source: See table 1.

Table 3
Ordinary Seamen's Wages Compared to National Means, Selected Ports, Foreign-Going Sail, 1850-1914
(National Mean for OSs = 100 in each year)

Year	Tø	K	Tr	R	Year	Tø	K	Tr	R
1850	98	N/A	103	N/A	1883	103	98	91	N/A
1851	99	N/A	102	N/A	1884	106	98	N/A	N/A
1852	100	N/A	100	N/A	1885	104	100	97	99
1853	100	94	107	N/A	1886	99	N/A	109	N/A
1854	103	100	100	N/A	1887	102	113	98	N/A
1855	96	116	93	N/A	1888	103	103	90	101
1856	101	104	95	N/A	1889	107	92	88	97
1857	100	106	98	N/A	1890	109	91	67	98
1858	95	115	111	N/A	1891	104	93	94	100
1859	99	99	110	N/A	1892	105	95	97	101
1860	98	101	110	N/A	1893	101	93	95	102
1861	100	100	118	N/A	1894	102	94	94	101
1862	100	103	120	N/A	1895	102	95	104	102
1863	100	108	115	N/A	1896	101	84	95	99
1864	102	100	110	100	1897	102	91	100	100
1865	102	104	103	98	1898	102	83	90	101
1866	104	107	104	98	1899	100	59	N/A	101
1867	100	109	108	99	1900	101	86	75	104
1868	100	118	96	102	1901	N/A	N/A	N/A	102
1869	99	115	N/A	104	1902	101	N/A	N/A	103
1870	99	115	108	N/A	1903	100	N/A	N/A	105
1871	99	110	124	N/A	1904	102	N/A	N/A	103
1872	99	N/A	103	N/A	1905	99	N/A	N/A	102
1873	104	N/A	91	N/A	1906	99	152	72	100
1874	106	N/A	99	N/A	1907	99	99	93	105
1875	100	95	97	N/A	1908	98	95	88	100
1876	101	103	97	N/A	1909	95	158	85	101
1877	101	103	92	105	1910	92	93	81	102
1878	100	97	108	106	1911	94	N/A	81	96
1879	99	116	101	106	1912	93	N/A	56	105
1880	99	99	106	106	1913	95	N/A	64	97
1881	101	N/A	97	106	1914	89	124	76	99
1882	103	106	93	101					

Notes: See table 1.

Source: See table 1.

Table 4
Cooks' Wages Compared to National Means, Selected Ports, Foreign-Going Sail, 1850-1914
(National Mean for Cooks = 100 in each year)

Year	Tø	K	Tr	R	Year	Tø	K	Tr	R
1850	115	99	100	N/A	1883	98	105	99	N/A
1851	109	97	103	N/A	1884	101	107	N/A	N/A
1852	114	107	100	N/A	1885	99	89	N/A	88
1853	122	107	104	N/A	1886	91	154	135	N/A
1854	121	100	104	N/A	1887	89	N/A	117	N/A
1855	109	102	99	N/A	1888	85	120	70	93
1856	119	101	92	N/A	1889	97	102	75	99
1857	113	100	92	N/A	1890	124	113	73	103
1858	105	102	101	N/A	1891	104	102	64	119
1859	107	100	100	N/A	1892	108	127	146	125
1860	105	94	106	N/A	1893	111	95	101	106
1861	106	100	106	N/A	1894	102	85	106	109
1862	109	100	108	N/A	1895	124	125	N/A	113
1863	104	105	101	N/A	1896	104	N/A	109	122
1864	112	107	105	87	1897	102	77	N/A	125
1865	116	108	101	86	1898	106	109	N/A	136
1866	115	113	85	77	1899	114	82	110	96
1867	118	115	103	81	1900	104	89	66	150
1868	110	129	123	86	1901	N/A	N/A	203	89
1869	114	115	148	96	1902	98	N/A	N/A	105
1870	100	136	103	N/A	1903	105	N/A	77	112
1871	111	115	98	N/A	1904	108	N/A	N/A	100
1872	104	185	96	N/A	1905	126	N/A	N/A	132
1873	115	69	88	N/A	1906	125	98	N/A	128
1874	107	N/A	145	N/A	1907	120	N/A	94	131
1875	108	111	111	N/A	1908	118	152	105	152
1876	107	125	96	N/A	1909	155	172	N/A	115
1877	105	126	110	85	1910	89	89	N/A	96
1878	99	95	91	86	1911	133	N/A	N/A	115
1879	99	122	123	89	1912	183	N/A	N/A	80
1880	92	N/A	119	87	1913	184	N/A	N/A	N/A
1881	99	N/A	92	96	1914	95	284	N/A	N/A
1882	102	123	88	94					

Notes: See table 1.

Source: See table 1.

An examination of table 1, which depicts the wages of first mates, suggests that in the 1850s rates were consistently above the national average in Tønsberg, while in Trondheim, the only other port among our sample for which we have a reliable time series for this decade, wages were below the national mean in seven of the ten years. On average, first mates recruited in Tønsberg were paid about three percent more than the national mean during the decade, while those who enlisted in Trondheim were paid about four percent below prevailing national wages.

But equally important, these differentials were not consistent. Mean wages in Tønsberg dipped below the national mean in 1866 and remained there for most of the next two decades. Tønsberg mates lost their premium in the 1860s (on average, they were paid at the national mean over the decade), and in both the 1870s and 1880s they received on average three percent less than those recruited elsewhere. But after 1889 the picture was altered once again: in no year through 1913 did Tønsberg mates fall below the national scale. The mean differentials were three percent in the 1890s, two percent between 1900 and 1909, and four percent in the final quinquennium before World War I.

The other port in the southern part of the country is Risør. If there were at least regional markets for this class of labour, we would expect to see a pattern closely resembling Tønsberg. But in fact the experience in this town was almost exactly the reverse of what I have just described in Tønsberg. In the 1860s, Risør wages for first mates were two percent below the national average (Tønsberg was at the national mean); in the 1870s, while mates' remuneration in Risør reached the national mean, Tønsberg's was declining. Risør wages for mates did not, however, remain so high. In the 1880s, mean wages averaged two percent below the national average (compared to three percent in Tønsberg), and in the next two decades Risør mates were paid three percent below the mean (Tønsberg was three and two percent, respectively, above national norms). In the final half-decade prior to the First World War, Risør mates earned monthly wages one percent above the national average, about three percent below the rates in Tønsberg.

The two more northerly ports were Trondheim and Kristiansund. We can examine wages for mates in the former throughout the period, but data are available during only four decades (the 1860s through the 1890s) for the latter. For the most part, wages in Trondheim stayed below national levels until the 1880s (by four, one and three percent per decade). They rose in the 1880s to an average of three percent above the country-wide figure; declined to one percent below in the 1890s; were at the national mean in the first decade of the twentieth century; and were six percent below Norwegian norms in the last five years before the war. The experience is Kristiansund was different in significant respects.

Wages for mates were four percent below the Trondheim level in the 1860s, one percent lower in the 1870s and three percent less in the 1880s. Remuneration for mates recruited in Kristiansund reached the national mean only in the 1880s.

The key point that these data show is that for mates none of the ports was consistently characterized by either high or low wages. In each port monthly wages reached or exceeded the national average in at least one decade; similarly, all were below national means for at least two ten-year periods. On average, we can call Tønsberg by Norwegian standards a high wage port for mates; the other three could properly be called low wage. But as the data show, this type of designation needs to be qualified: for whatever reasons, the patterns were far too diverse to be subject to simplistic classification.

What about carpenters, our surrogates for skilled maritime labour? Were the patterns outlined for mates similar or different? Indexed data similar to that provided for mates depict the wage experiences of carpenters (see table 2) and show that while there were some similarities, especially in long-term trends, the more specific patterns of wage growth in the individual ports were in important ways dissimilar to what was observed for mates.

The patterns in Tønsberg were perhaps the most similar for the two occupations; indeed, if we use the relationship of local wages to national norms as a criterion, the only difference appears in the 1880s, in which mates' wages were below national means while carpenters were one percent above. But the most significant differences occurred after 1890. Mates were between two and four percent above national means in each decade, but for carpenters the premiums ranged from six to fourteen percent. In relative terms, at least, Tønsberg's skilled workers appear to have fared better than did officers recruited in the town.

Similar to what we noted for mates, skilled workers in Risør experienced a virtual mirror image of the patterns in Tønsberg. Relative wages in the south coast port declined from being five percent above national standards in the 1860s to six percent below in the 1900s. The difference between Risør and Tønsberg was perhaps most evident after 1890: the latter, as we have seen, enjoyed sizable premiums, but in Risør carpenters' pay was from two to six percent below national norms.

Trondheim was for the most part a low-wage port for carpenters, exhibiting patterns that were less mixed than for mates. Only in the 1860s did wages exceed national norms, and even then by only one percent over the decade. The 1880s and 1890s were in relative terms particularly bad, with wages falling six and seven percent below national averages, respectively. Compared with mates, carpenters came closer to national averages in the 1850s, 1860s and 1870s (by two percent in each decade), but thereafter fared more poorly. Mates were closer to the national means for their occupations by nine percent in the 1880s, six percent in the 1890s, and two percent between 1900 and 1909.

Finally, we come to Kristiansund, which for carpenters provided an exceedingly erratic wage environment. For three of the six periods that we can measure, Kristiansund carpenters were above the national norm — by as much as seven percent on average in the 1870s. But the town was also well below national standards in some decades, especially in the 1890s when wages averaged ten percent less than elsewhere in Norway. If we compare carpenters to mates, we can also see some important differences, especially in the 1870s (a difference of eleven percent in favour of carpenters compared to national means) and the 1890s (an eight percent relative advantage to mates).

The wage experiences of carpenters in the four ports for the most part reinforce what we noted about mates. In every port, carpenters enjoyed wage premiums in at least one decade; likewise they all were below the mean at least once. Tønsberg paid on average relatively high wages, while Trondheim for the most part fell below the national mean. In Kristiansund and Risør the trends were more mixed, although on average both fell slightly below national averages. But it is worth reiterating that the patterns were significantly different, even if in some ways the various ports' wage histories exhibit some similarities.

Ordinary seamen (OSs) were deckhands who lacked specific skills. Unlike able-bodied seamen (ABs), they did not possess the training to work the sails, although there is no shortage of evidence of masters sending OSs aloft in even the worst weather.[16] OSs were for the most part younger than ABs and in many cases had little or no experience at sea.[17] Nonetheless, many of their tasks were similar to those performed by ABs, and shipowners frequently preferred to hire lower-

---

[16]See, for example, Burton, "Apprenticeship Regulation," for a discussion not only of the practice of sending OSs and boys up the masts but also for a statistical analysis of the consequences.

[17]The characteristics of OSs are discussed in Fischer, "The Sea as Highway." This essay also contains a lengthy analysis of another characteristic of OSs: their propensity to desert from sailing vessels.

cost OSs while reducing the number of more skilled (and expensive) ABs. For this reason, an examination of their wage environment is a reasonable way of looking at the experiences of deckhands (see table 3). Even a brief glance at the time series suggests yet another variation on the theme outlined above for mates and carpenters.

In Tønsberg, OSs were paid above national levels in the four decades between 1860 and the turn of the century, but below national norms in the other three periods. The difference between OSs on the one hand, and mates and carpenters on the other, were especially noticeable in the 1850s, 1870s, 1900s and the final quinquennium before the war. In the 1870s, Tønsberg OSs were on average paid above national levels, while for the other two categories, labour was compensated above prevailing Norwegian averages. In the other three periods, the reverse was true (Tønsberg OSs were below national levels while mates and carpenters were above). But for the most part, OSs enrolled in Tønsberg were close to national standards, never diverging by more than three percent in any decade until 1910 (they diverged by seven percent in the final five years under study).

This once again was very different than in Risør, the port which was closest geographically. Indeed, Risør OSs represent one of only two unequivocal cases in this study: in every decade, OSs who joined vessels in this port were paid at or above national levels, sometimes by as much as six percent (in the 1870s). As a high-wage port for this type of labour, it obviously was different yet again from Tønsberg, the most obvious harbour for comparison.

Trondheim was exceedingly different than either. OSs did well in relative terms if they served before 1880: in each of the three first decades, they were paid above national norms, by two percent in the 1850s and 1870s and by nine percent in the 1860s. But thereafter conditions altered sharply, and Trondheim became for OSs an extremely low-wage port. Deckhands of this type were paid below the national average by three percent in the 1880s, eight percent in the 1890s, seventeen percent in the 1900s, and a staggering twenty-eight percent in the years 1910-1914. While the pattern was mixed, the amplitude of the differences after 1880 make it fair to characterize Trondheim as a low-wage port.

It is less easy, however, to categorize Kristiansund. In a previous study of ABs, Helge Nordvik and I noted that deckhands in this west coast port had very different experiences than those recruited elsewhere in Norway.[18] The evidence in table 3, while showing a different pattern than for ABs, does little to alter this conclusion. OSs were generally paid significantly more in Kristiansund than the national average, reaching a high of eighteen percent above the country-wide mean for those years that we can measure in the 1900s. But the experiences in that decade provide a striking example of the instability of the labour market in this port. In 1906, for example, the twenty-three men who signed on as OSs received about fifty-two percent more than the national average (with a low standard deviation around the mean), yet the next year they were **below** the Norwegian mean (again with a low standard deviation for the thirty-one cases collected). Indeed, a comparison of the decade 1900-1909 with the previous ten-year span, in which wages were twelve percent below national averages, makes the same point.

To summarize, OSs' wages provide not only a clear example of a consistently high-wage port but also one of the best cases of wage instability (Kristiansund). Tønsberg wages were about average, while Trondheim's were below national scales. It remains difficult to designate high- or low-wage ports with precision or to find consistent wage differentials.

Finally, we can turn our attention to cooks. Compared to the British and Canadian merchant marines, cooks in the Norwegian fleet were drastically underpaid relative to other labour. As table 4 shows, they also had the most unstable labour market of any of the categories of labour under consideration. All four ports were characterized by wild short- and long-term fluctuations. None of the labour markets was especially stable, on this criterion differing only in the degree of their swings. And contrary to my expectations, all were less stable after 1900 than before.

If there were a relatively stable port for cooks, it was Tønsberg. Wages were consistently above average through 1877, generally below the national means in the 1880s, and above average thereafter. In the 1850s, cooks who signed-on to sailing vessels in the port received about thirteen percent more than those who joined elsewhere in the nation, a differential which would have been noteworthy for other categories of labour but which was hardly atypical for cooks. In the next decade, the premium declined to twelve percent and fell further to six percent in the 1870s. Tønsberg was five percent below national norms in the 1880s, but

---

[18]See Fischer and Nordvik, "Norwegian *Matroser*."

recovered to ten percent above in the 1890s, eighteen percent in the 1900s, and thirty-seven percent between 1910 and 1914. It is also worth noting the wild gyrations in mean wages after 1900, especially from 1909 onward. And it is also worth reiterating that in all these years I have substantial numbers of cases and low standard deviations around the mean.

Risør, like Tønsberg, exhibited instability in the latter part of the period but was unlike its sister port in the pattern of wages relative to national means. It was a consistently low-wage port through the 1880s, with cooks never reaching the national average until 1890. In being consistently below the national mean for this period, cooks were atypical of any other occupation in Risør. Wages recovered relative to national statistics in the 1890s, a decade in which Risør cooks enjoyed on average a fifteen percent premium, and the 1900s (an average of twenty-one percent above national figures). The yearly fluctuations, however, were just as wild as in Tønsberg, with the most glaring examples in the years 1898-1901.

Cooks recruited in Trondheim did better relative to national wages than any other category of labour examined in the port; wages for cooks were above average in every decade except the 1880s. But what is especially worth noting is the amplitude of the annual swings, which outstripped anything in either Tønsberg or Risør. No other port ever had a year in which wages were so far below the national mean (thirty-six percent in 1891), and only Kristiansund ever enjoyed a year in which wages were so far above levels elsewhere (more than double national rates in 1901).

It should occasion little surprise that the port with the most dramatic swings was Kristiansund. On average, this town was above the national average in every period, but it is questionable how much worth decadal means are when wages could swing between eleven percent below national averages and 184% above in the same period, as they did between 1910 and 1914. Indeed, these kinds of patterns characterized every decade from the 1870s. It is perhaps fitting that the most unstable port and the most unstable job should have this kind of conjunction.

What all these data underscore is the point I made at the outset. Regional differences existed, but they were neither concentrated in specific areas nor were they consistent. Perhaps this is not surprising on one level; after all, more than most occupations, those in the maritime sector likely responded in part to trends beyond the borders either of the nation or of a specific community. But on the other hand, that they existed at all suggests that wage levels were determined only in part exogenously. Despite a wealth of Norwegian local histories, there has been too little research on the local landward economies – and especially on local labour markets – for me to hazard a guess as to why the specific differentials discussed actually existed. But there is one thing the data do suggest: if there were national labour markets (wage equalization), the patterns were not consistent.

Unfortunately, testing for national labour markets is not as simple as might first appear. The initial difficulty is in determining the criteria by which to judge whether markets were integrated (or moving in that direction). For the most part, economic historians have tended to look for relationships between markets, a condition most easily tested using correlations. When they have wished to be especially precise, they have correlated first differences (the yearly variations rather than the raw numbers). While there is nothing wrong with either procedure, it is as well to be cognizant of the pitfalls. If wage equalization has any meaning, it suggests that levels ought to be converging. Yet common sense suggests that this can lead to **negative** correlations, especially if convergence were achieved because one port's wages declined while another's rose.[19]

The other problem with correlations is that they do not take fully into account wage levels. Again, although it may seem obvious that integrated markets should not have major discrepancies in remuneration levels, correlations are principally measures of movements or trends rather than levels. For example, to obtain a perfect correlation of +1.0, the two (or more) variables need only to move up (or down) by the same number of units per period of time. To choose an apocryphal example, let us assume that a seaman in port A was paid one kroner per month in year X, while a seaman in port B was paid one hundred kroner per month in the same year. Then let us assume that in year Y the wages were two kroner and 101 kroner, and in year Z three kroner and 102 kroner, respectively. The correlation coefficient for this example would be a perfect +1.0, but it would be ludicrous to suggest that the markets

---

[19]For full discussions of this phenomenon, see Fischer, "International Maritime Labour;" Fischer, "Seamen in a Space Economy: International Regional Patterns of Maritime Wages on Sailing Vessels, 1863-1900," in H.E.S. Fisher (ed.), *Lisbon as a Port Town, the British Seaman and Other Maritime Themes* (Exeter, 1988), 57-92.

were integrating. It is also worth noting that in this example the correlation of first differences would be identical.

Of course, the problem highlighted by this example could be remedied to a degree by calculating growth rates. These would indicate that the underlying trends were in fact different (a compound annual growth rate of 73.2% per year in port A versus just under one percent per year in port B). But by itself, this does not tell us if markets were integrating. To see why not, it is worth recalling Nikita Krushchev's famous boast in the mid-1950s that Soviet GNP would overtake that of the United States within a decade because the growth rate was higher. While it might have seemed that way looking at growth rates, unless they are put into their proper context, growth rates can also be misleading indicators of integration.

I have no simple answer to these problems. In trying to measure wage equalization in Norway I have adopted a number of different procedures. I have calculated standard correlations (using both the raw numbers and first differences) and run a series of regressions to estimate the compound annual growth rates of all wages; some of the results will be reported below. But I also use two other techniques. One involves correlations, but utilizes the index numbers in tables 1 to 4 rather than either raw numbers or first differences. A little thought will suggest why this approach has its uses. Like any correlation, this one takes cognizance of trends, but because the numbers are indexed to national means, it also takes into account relative levels. A perfectly integrated market would yield continuous index numbers of 100, although it would be impossible to calculate a correlation coefficient (this is because there would be no increments). But in an imperfect world, such a result will never occur. Instead, by correlating the various pairs of ports, all of which have been deflated by the same index number in a given year, we can derive a useful **single** measure of integration. In reality, of course, this is a form of multiple correlation, with the underlying assumption that integration involves not only pairs of ports but also convergence with some kind of national average. There is only one caveat: while evidence of wage equalization can in theory yield either a positive of a negative coefficient, the pairs of variables **must** be converging on the national average (100) to demonstrate integration. This is another advantage of using the index numbers, since such trends are more easily seen with a base of one hundred than with raw values.

The other technique I use is what I call a measure of convergence. This is not a very sophisticated number; it is merely a growth rate of the index and is designed to show whether over any given period of time (decades, in this paper) the wage levels for a given occupation in a port are moving toward the national average. It has meaning, of course, only in the context of the point at which the calculation begins, but it does provide another clue about wage equalization.

Before reporting the results, it is useful to make three other points. First, I have not attempted to "smooth" the data by using moving averages. The principle reason for this is that nineteenth-century wages – at least in the maritime sector – moved in irregular waves. I have observed this trend in every market, both inside and outside Norway, that I have ever studied. Moving averages, of course, smooth out the waves, but given the patterns that existed, they often distort the results rather than reveal underlying trends, which is what they are supposed to do. The reason for this is that the trends for different occupations (or for individual markets) were seldom precisely the same. The second point is that because of the wave-like movements – and due to the extreme variability of some time series – I have not used interpolations of any kind. While this imposes limits on the analysis, it makes a good deal of sense since in many cases it is impossible to know what technique to use. The final point that needs to be made involves an explanation of why I use an artificial periodization – in this case, decades – rather than, say, investment or economic cycles. While I admit that using cycles would be preferable, I do not use them here because, as tables 1-4 make clear, the cycles are different in the various occupations and ports. Choosing one set of cycles rather than another introduces distortions; so too does the use of decades, but at least whatever distortion is injected into the analysis is consistent rather than biased toward one or another port or occupation.

With these considerations in mind we can look at the evidence, beginning with first mates. We have already seen that the patterns of nominal wages in each port were different. But is there evidence of a **trend** toward wage equalization? The evidence is at best mixed. While the growth rates move in the same direction for every decade and port (see table 5), for those ports in which we can measure the growth rates, they vary widely, especially prior to 1890. But in that decade (and in the first decade of the twentieth century) the growth rates for Tønsberg and Risør were relatively close to the national averages. The regression lines used to estimate the growth rates, however, were poor fits for the 1890s, but very good measures for the years 1900-1909.[20]

Table 5
Compound Annual Growth Rates of First Mates' Wages, 1850-1914

Decade	Tønsberg	Kristiansund	Trondheim	Risør	Norway
1850-59	N/A	N/A	+2.44%	N/A	+1.90%
1860-69	+0.51%	N/A	+0.82	N/A	+1.10
1870-79	+0.72	N/A	+1.87	N/A	+0.84
1880-89	+0.81	N/A	N/A	N/A	+0.26
1890-99	+0.21	N/A	N/A	+0.13%	+0.29
1900-09	+3.28	N/A	N/A	+2.95	+2.54
1910-14	+6.28	N/A	+2.64	+9.57	+9.67

Notes: All growth rates are calculated using linear regressions of the form Log Y = a + bt. Rates for Trondheim in the 1860s are for 1860-1868 and in the 1870s for 1872-1879. Tønsberg growth rates in the 1900s are for 1902-1909.

Source: See table 1.

Calculations of correlation coefficients suggest that the ports in the 1890s look less similar than the growth rates suggest but reinforce the notion that there was a quantitative difference before and after 1900. In the 1850s, no pair of ports correlated with any other at a higher value than +.47. The next decade was slightly better, but only two pairs (Kristiansund-Risør and Risør-Norway) yielded values in excess of +.44, and both Tønsberg-Kristiansund and Tønsberg-Risør yielded negative values. Similar patterns existed in the 1870s and 1880s, with one serious

---

[20] The correlation coefficients of the regressions prior to 1890 never exceed +.49 for Tønsberg or +.68 for Trondheim. Indeed, even the Norwegian means seldom show good correlations; with the exception of the 1860s (+.92), the coefficients never exceeded +.44 period to 1890. The growth rates for the 1890s, however, give reason to worry about how good a description of growth the least-squares line represents, since the coefficients were all exceptionally low (+.24 for Tønsberg; +.27 for Risør; and +.38 for Norway). But they are much better for the 1900-1909 period: +.91 for Tønsberg; +.89 for Risør; and +.89 for Norway. They are even higher for the last quinquennium before the war.

difference: in the first of these decades, all ports except Trondheim correlated above +.94 with the Norwegian average. But this relationship declined sharply in the 1880s, which suggests that any movement toward wage equalization was not sustained. This is bolstered by what the statistics show for the 1890s: over half of the correlations were negative, and two ports (Kristiansund and Trondheim) had strongly negative correlations with the national average. But the period after 1900 was characterized by strong positive coefficients, especially between the two southern ports and the Norwegian means.[21]

But the other two statistics suggest some caution in concluding that there was a strong movement toward equalization in mates' wages after 1900. In the decade 1900-1909, for example, the indexed values for Tønsberg and Risør correlated at only +.49 and at +.34 for the 1910-1914 period. The growth rates (-.18% and -2.66% for Tønsberg and +.42% and -.30% for Risør) support the notion that whatever integration was occurring was weaker than the earlier statistics might suggest.

In short, the evidence implies that whatever wage equalization was occurring in the labour market for first mates was confined to the southern part of the country and, temporally, after 1900. Moreover, the trend was not very strong. Even on the eve of the First World War, patterns in Tønsberg and Risør were still obviously being influenced by different factors. Missing data for the early twentieth century makes it difficult to say anything very precise about Trondheim and Kristiansund, except that the available evidence provides no reason to believe that any type of equalization was taking place during this period.

What about the labour market for carpenters? Here the initial evidence looks more promising. Table 6 summarizes the growth rates, which depict a much closer (and much earlier) congruence than we saw with mates. In almost every case (with the exception of the 1890s) the regression equations yielded better fits as well, which mean that the growth rates are likely a better description of wage trends than they were for mates.

The growth rates direct our attention to two decades in particular: the 1850s and the 1900s. The correlations show very high values in the first decade (all pairs that we can calculate were above +.93 except for Trondheim-Kristiansund, which were +.65). The coefficients were

---

[21]Tønsberg and Risør correlated at +.94 and +.98, respectively; Tønsberg-Norway at +.99 and +.97; and Risør-Norway at +.97 and +.99.

lower in the 1860s for every pair except for Trondheim-Kristiansund. But a remarkable thing happened in the 1870s: the correlations were higher than for any other decade for this particular occupation: all were at least +.85 and most were above +.94. It would be tempting – but I believe wrong – to interpret this as a positive sign of wage equalization. There are a variety of reasons for this, including much lower correlations using the index,[22] but the principle rationale for viewing the 1870s as deviant rather than suggestive of new conditions is what happened in the next decade, when only three pairs, all involving the two southern ports and the Norwegian average, were above +.65. The 1890s were even worse: the same three pairs were all related above +.80 (although all were substantially weaker than in the 1880s), but every correlation with Trondheim was negative, and two of the four with Kristiansund were also negative.[23]

Table 6
Compound Annual Growth Rates of Carpenters' Wages,
1850-1914

Decade	Tønsberg	Kristiansund	Trondheim	Risør	Norway
1850-59	+2.85%	+2.11%	+2.12%	N/A	+2.51%
1860-69	+1.94	+3.08	+0.87	+1.26%	+1.91
1870-79	+1.67	N/A	+2.12	N/A	+1.63
1880-89	+1.57	+2.13	N/A	N/A	+0.84
1890-99	+0.02	-2.94	N/A	-0.15	-0.29
1900-09	+0.91	N/A	N/A	+0.46	+1.14
1910-14	+3.69	N/A	N/A	+9.90	+6.64

Notes: Tønsberg growth rates for 1900-1909 are for 1902-1909; Kristiansund for the 1880s are for 1880-1885 and for the 1890s for 1890-1896; Risør for the 1860s are for 1862-1867.

Source: See table 1.

---

[22]The correlations with the indexed numbers were all under +.56 in the 1870s.

[23]Lest their be any suggestion that the negative correlations might be indicative of the formation of a market between Trondheim and Kristiansund, it should be noted that the correlation between these two ports in the 1890s was -.37.

It is impossible to carry any analysis involving Kristiansund and Trondheim into the twentieth century. But there are sufficient data to enable us to examine Tønsberg and Risør. The growth rates after 1900 were roughly similar, but the correlations do not suggest any serious wage equalization: between 1900 and 1909, for example, Risør and Tønsberg correlated only at a disappointing +.28. Tønsberg was closely related to Norwegian trends in both periods (+.87 in the 1900s and +.97 in the years 1910-1914), but Risør resembled the national movements less strongly (+.61 in the 1900s, improving to a much stronger +.83, 1910-1914). This conclusion is borne out by the indices as well, especially for the 1900-1909 period. The two ports exhibited almost no correlation (+.02); while the growth rates were relatively similar (-.73% for Tønsberg and -.63% for Risør), all this shows is that while Tønsberg was moving toward the national mean, Risør was moving away from it.

If there were any real wage equalization for maritime carpenters, it existed early in the period rather than later. By every measure we have, the strong relationships between the various ports weakened consistently after the 1870s. While it is possible to envisage labour market fragmentation, everything we know about nineteenth-century Norway suggests that this did not occur. A more reasonable conclusion would be that there never was anything resembling real wage equalization for ships' carpenters prior to the First World War.

We may now turn our attention to OSs. To the extent that any type of labour examined in this paper benefitted from a market broader than merely an individual locality, it was the ordinary seamen. The evidence suggests at least regional wage equalization in southern Norway (Tønsberg and Risør) by the 1870s. It does not, however, point to the existence of any national market (see table 7).

With the exception of the 1890s, all growth rates in every period were positive. But more important, from the 1870s they converged, especially for the southern ports. This clue is supported by the correlations, which are moderate for the 1850s and 1860s, but stronger thereafter. Indeed, Tønsberg and Risør never had a relationship weaker than +.92 after 1870. The coefficients between the southern ports and Kristiansund were mixed, while with Trondheim they were consistently either close to zero or negative. The correlations and the growth rates based upon the index show convergence in the 1870s as well; while they are weaker than might have been expected for the 1880s, they consistently point to some degree of wage equalization thereafter.

Table 7
Compound Annual Growth Rates of Ordinary Seamen's Wages, 1850-1914

Decade	Tønsberg	Kristiansund	Trondheim	Risør	Norway
1850-59	+2.77%	+0.61%	+3.20%	N/A	+2.94%
1860-69	+1.44	+2.80	+0.08	+0.04%	+1.33
1870-79	+1.34	N/A	+0.25	N/A	+1.29
1880-89	+1.49	N/A	N/A	N/A	+1.20
1890-99	-1.16	-3.18	+0.62	-0.49	-0.60
1900-09	+1.57	N/A	N/A	+0.59	+0.83
1910-14	+4.68	N/A	+1.25	+4.52	+5.02

Notes: Tønsberg growth rates for the 1900s are for 1902-1909; Kristiansund growth rates for the 1850s are for 1853-1859; Trondheim growth rates in the 1860s cover the years 1860-1868 and for the 1890s are for 1890-1898; Risør rates for the 1860s are for 1864-1869 only.

Source: See table 1.

Finally, we come to cooks. Because, as we have already seen, even the local markets for cooks were so unstable, I am not going to present any growth rates, since the regressions used to calculate them were consistently poor fits. Given what we have already seen about cooks, it is no surprise that there was no evidence of wage equalization. As I pointed out above, cooks in Norway were treated differently than elsewhere. But further work on the question must be done before we can venture any conclusions about why they should have been the most deviant of the occupations.

To summarize, the evidence suggests that only for OSs was there any solid evidence for wage equalization, and this was purely regional. For mates, I believe that there is some evidence (albeit less strong than for OSs) of something that looks like wage integration in the south after 1900. For carpenters, there is some superficial evidence of equalization early in the period, but whatever convergence had occurred fragmented by the 1880s. For cooks, there is no evidence of any trend toward wage equalization at any time or in any region.

The Efficiency of Maritime Labour Markets in the Age of Sail

Equalization of Supply and Demand

The wage data examined thus far of course concerned only labour that manned sailing vessels. But the Norwegian research project also yielded large amounts of evidence about those who served on steamers. Although Norway made the transition from sail to steam later than some nations, the balance clearly shifted in the first decade of the twentieth century. Professor Kindleberger believes – I think, sensibly – that an efficient market ought to be able to adapt fairly quickly to changes induced by exogenous variables, such as technological change.

To see how well Norwegian markets adapted, I want here to look at one specific port: Kristiania. I have not thus far examined in this paper the maritime labour market in Norway's capital and largest urban centre, chiefly because I only possess a continuous time series for the period from 1899. However, this is perfect for examining the way the market adapted to the introduction of steam. Moreover, there are sufficient cases that we can have confidence that the means reflect the state of the market. Table 8 shows these data for five categories of labour found on both sail and steam-powered vessels: first and second mates, ABs, OSs and cooks.

The trends reflected by the data are at best mixed. If we examine the experience of first mates, it appears that the market operated relatively efficiently. In 1899, for instance, first mates on steamers were paid more than eighteen kroner per month more for service in steam than their counterparts in sail, while by 1914 the difference had narrowed to less than one kroner. Since first mates' performed virtually the same tasks in steam and sail and generally had no responsibility for the propulsion system, a mate should have been able to move from sail to steam (and *vice versa*) with relative ease. Within fifteen years the market adjusted to reflect this reality.

Unfortunately, the markets for the other forms of labour in Kristiania did not function the same way. While the premium for second mates narrowed over time, it was once again increasing by 1914. ABs were initially paid less for service on steamers, a condition that was rational **if** the vessels were not auxiliaries, where the ability to climb the mast and work the sails might well have led to a premium. But by 1914 ABs on steamers were paid **more** than on sailing vessels; indeed, the steam increment for ABs was larger than for either category of mates. While there was never much difference in pay for OSs who served on steamers, there was also no discernable trend to suggest convergence over time. And for cooks, we can see that, far from adjusting, the markets actually diverged sharply over the period.[24]

Table 8
Steam Increments in Kristiania, 1899-1914
(NOK per month)

Year	First Mates	Second Mates	Able-Bodied Seamen	OSs	Cooks
1899	+18.05	+7.64	-5.38	-1.10	+12.28
1900	+16.04	+3.58	-4.74	-2.31	+ 9.20
1901	+18.83	+3.14	-5.27	-2.18	+3.46
1902	+22.22	+6.42	+0.56	-0.70	+8.24
1903	+22.31	+8.88	-1.21	-0.27	+8.65
1904	+18.97	+8.84	-1.09	-0.98	+6.76
1905	+21.37	+9.29	+0.19	-0.26	+11.21
1906	+18.16	+5.08	-2.54	-0.79	+11.27
1907	+12.73	+1.94	-3.06	-1.88	+8.46
1908	+15.62	+5.69	-1.43	-0.14	+16.71
1909	+18.52	+4.69	+1.79	+0.12	+14.46
1910	+13.81	+2.87	-0.19	-0.18	+16.04
1911	+14.55	+4.87	+2.43	-0.85	+19.67
1912	+8.81	-1.84	+5.35	-0.02	+17.34
1913	+5.53	+4.50	+4.50	-0.91	+23.22
1914	+0.82	+5.12	+6.50	-0.78	+26.68

Note: Data represent the average premium paid for service on steamers.

Source: See table 1.

If there were not consistent adaptation in maritime labour markets, it is also notable that there was little convergence with landward labour markets in the same trades. This is shown clearly in table 9, which depicts the markets for firemen recruited in Kristiania for both steamers and the railroad. The two ought to have been related since the

---

[24]It might be argued that the reason that cooks were paid so much better on steamers was a function of the higher proportion of steam passenger vessels. Doubtless there is some truth to this contention, but the divergence shown in table 8 must also say something about the way the labour market worked. I make this judgement because similar patterns existed in most Norwegian ports, regardless of whether they were served by large numbers of passenger liners or not.

tasks performed were basically the same, as were the skills required.[25] Yet the data do not depict an adaptable market. In 1899 firemen on the railway were paid about thirty-nine kroner per month more than their compatriots who served in the merchant marine. Far from converging, the gap actually rose over the next decade and one-half, with the trend especially obvious after 1910. By 1914, railway firemen were paid about 110 kroner per month more than those who worked at sea. This is also reflected in the simple correlation coefficient between the two series, which was a disappointing +.24.

On balance, with a few notable exceptions, Kristiania's labour markets do not appear over time to have adapted well to the introduction of steam. If this judgement is correct, it is difficult to be too sanguine about the efficiency of Norwegian maritime labour markets prior to World War I.

Employment Stability

The data available to me does not enable the creation of a data set to test employment stability as directly as we might like. Nonetheless, there is sufficient evidence to argue strongly that if stability is an important indicator of market efficiency, Norwegian maritime markets were not terribly efficient prior to 1914. The issue of stability has two sides: first, whether labour employed in the market was guaranteed long-term employment; and second, whether a buyer of labour could have some degree of confidence that the seller would make a long-term commitment. The question of what is meant by "long-term," so often a problem for economic historians, is no particular problem here, for reasons that will be clear in a moment.

---

[25]They should not, however, have been identical, since the career paths on the railroads and at sea were different. A fireman on a steamer was unlikely ever to advance; as long as he went to sea, he was likely to be a fireman. On the railroads, on the other hand, the job of fireman was often a stepping stone to becoming an engine driver. I am grateful to Peter Davies for reminding me of this. Nonetheless, because the skills required were broadly similar, I still believe that the comparison in table 9 has at least some suggestive power. For some evidence about the relationship between landward and seaward markets for carpenters in Norway, see the discussions in Lewis R. Fischer and Helge W. Nordvik, "Salaries of the Sea: Maritime Wages in Stavanger, 1892-1914," *Stavanger Historisk Årbok 1987* (Stavanger, 1988), 103-132; and Fischer and Nordvik, "Fish and Ships: The Social Structure of the Maritime Labour Force in Haugesund in the 1870s," *Sjøfartshistorisk Årbok 1986* (Bergen, 1987), 139-170.

Table 9
Firemen's Wages Compared to Manufacturing Wages,
Kristiania, 1899-1914
(NOK per month)

Year	Firemen (Sea)	Fireman (Rail)
1899	49.05	88.08
1900	49.50	91.68
1901	48.57	92.88
1902	48.41	92.64
1903	48.65	93.60
1904	47.71	94.80
1905	48.42	92.88
1906	49.93	94.80
1907	51.70	102.72
1908	56.95	102.00
1909	53.99	120.00
1910	55.12	122.40
1911	58.02	127.84
1912	66.36	148.25
1913	71.85	187.20
1914	74.20	184.30

Sources: Firemen (sea), see table 1; Firemen (rail), NHH, WA 58.

The first issue – whether there were any long-term guarantees to labour – can be answered simply. We have enough samples of Norwegian crew agreements to know that prior to World War I buyers sought labour only for the short-term. Most agreements were for the voyage, as they were in the British Empire as well. Moreover, most agreements specified maximum time limits for service, most often one to three years. We have not, however, located enough of these documents for steamers or liners to know whether the same held true in those sectors. But for sailing labour, it is clear that there were no guarantees of long-term employment.[26]

The evidence regarding the second issue – the commitment by seamen – is even more overwhelmingly negative. Norwegian seamen

---

[26]Fischer and Nordvik, "From Namsos to Halden," 54-55.

showed just about the highest propensity to desert of any national group on sailing vessels. Indeed, it was so bad that the Norwegian government on several occasions commissioned studies of the problem in the domestically-owned fleet.[27] And when Norwegians served on foreign-flag vessels – as they did in large numbers – they also had an extraordinarily high rate of desertion, often as high as sixty percent in some North American locales.[28] While the issue of desertion is complex, it is clear from the record that few Norwegian seamen were especially interested in making a long-term commitment to a particular vessel or owner – or, indeed, even to life at sea.[29]

Conclusion

The data presented here do not provide a great deal of support for the notion that markets functioned efficiently in the three-quarters of a century before the outbreak of the Great War. Although it appears that most seamen entered the labour market of their own free will (at least if a perceived lack of alternative opportunities is not considered compulsion), on the other three criteria suggested by Kindleberger the picture is less favourable. Overall, there is little evidence of consistent spatial integration over time. The evidence on market adaptability, while more mixed, does not lend overwhelming support to the notion that markets efficiently allocated resources with the advent of steam. Similarly, there was little integration between landward and seaward labour markets even when the type of labour involved was similar. Finally, there is virtually no evidence to point to a commitment toward employment stability, either on the part of management or labour.

---

[27]Helge W. Nordvik, "Norwegian Sailors in the Canadian Merchant Marine, 1863-1914: A Preliminary Survey," in Einar Hope (ed.), *Studies in Shipping Economics Presented to Professor Arnljot Strømme Svendsen* (Oslo, 1982), 79-86.

[28]For a more thorough analysis, see Lewis R. Fischer and Helge W. Nordvik, "A Crucial Six Percent: Norwegian Sailors in the Canadian Merchant Marine, 1863-1913," *Sjøfartshistorisk Årbok 1984* (Bergen, 1985), 139-159.

[29]The most comprehensive analysis of nineteenth-century desertion is Lewis R. Fischer, "A Dereliction of Duty: The Problem of Desertion on Nineteenth Century Sailing Vessels," in Rosemary Ommer and Gerald Panting (eds.), *Working Men Who Got Wet* (St. John's, 1980), 51-70.

In short, the Norwegian evidence suggests that by modern standards Norwegian maritime labour markets performed fairly inefficiently after 1850. Perhaps most disturbingly, it does not appear that most functioned more smoothly in 1914 than two-thirds of a century earlier. While we obviously need more comparative studies, the Norwegian experience lends little support to the notion that maritime labour markets were efficient in the twilight of the age of sail.

The Danish Maritime Labour Market, 1880-1900

Morten Hahn-Pedersen and Poul Holm

Sailors' Wages in Eight North Sea Ports, 1863-1900

In his article "Around the Rim: Seamen's Wages in North Sea Ports, 1863-1900," Lewis R. Fischer challenged the notion that North Sea ports comprised an integrated maritime labour market. Fischer's analysis was based on a data set of 75,556 monthly wage agreements for able-bodied seamen (ABs) who joined sailing vessels in London, Dunkerque, Antwerp, Rotterdam, Hamburg, Copenhagen, Gothenburg and Tønsberg between 1863 and 1900. These showed that convergence between levels of pay was erratic and short-lived (see table 1). Only in the early 1880s and early 1890s did wage levels in the eight ports converge; in other years they varied considerably. Dunkerque and Tønsberg – and for almost half the time Gothenburg as well – generally paid less than London, while Hamburg and Rotterdam provided relatively high remuneration for most of the period. Fischer concluded that the lack of convergence refuted any thesis of increased integration of maritime labour markets around the North Sea.[1]

The considerable variation in wage levels between the ports prompts new questions. If there was no international convergence, what about national trends? Did shipowners and seamen take advantage of the variations and, if so, what does this tell us? From a Danish perspective, one interesting point in Fischer's data is that Copenhagen from 1893 until the end of the century was the port with the highest pay. This paper attempts to explain why this was so. To do this we analyze the demand side of the wage problem a little further, first within Fischer's North Sea

---

[1]Lewis R. Fischer, "Around the Rim: Seamen's Wages in North Sea Ports, 1863-1900," in Fischer, *et al.* (eds.), *The North Sea. Twelve Essays on the Social History of Maritime Labour* (Stavanger, 1992), 59-73.

context and then with special reference to Denmark, establishing a wage series for provincial ports. To broaden the concept of the maritime labour market, we then compare our findings with data for the booming fishery. Finally, we discuss whether there was a single Danish maritime labour market and suggest some directions for further research.

The Merchant Marine in Eight North Sea Nations, 1880-1900

Wages reflect the convergence of the supply and demand of labour and the relative bargaining power of employers and workers. The first industrial action for higher wages on Danish ships occurred in 1890, but the battle was lost. The Seamen's Union was founded only in 1897 and the first serious bargaining took place in 1898, when a minimum wage was agreed.[2] At this time wages paid ABs in Copenhagen were declining compared to provincial ports. In other words, sailors' bargaining power was weak and wages should thus reflect a relatively free market. If pay levels mirrored the pattern of demand, we would expect to find a correlation either with the development of the national merchant marine or total shipping clearances from specific ports.

The basic information on the development of the eight national merchant marines is presented in table 2. The French fleet underwent the highest growth over the two decades (98.1%, 1885-1900), followed by Germany (68%), Denmark (57.6%), Belgium (52%), Great Britain (39.4%), Sweden (11.2%), the Netherlands (5.5%), while Norway (0.7%) was stagnant.

The high wages of Hamburg, Copenhagen and Antwerp between 1880 and 1900 could be a result of the growth of national merchant marines. But this general explanation does not fit with the wage series nor does it explain why Copenhagen paid the highest wages from 1893 when the French and the German fleet was growing more rapidly. Looking specifically at growth between 1890-1900, even the logic is faulty. The Danish fleet expanded by thirty-four percent in this decade, which qualified for fourth place after Belgium (fifty percent), Germany (49.3%) and the Netherlands (35.7%). Looking only at the years in which Denmark had the highest maritime wages, the relative growth of the Danish fleet was surpassed by the Belgian and German merchant marines.

---

[2]Henning Vester Jørgensen, *Arbejdere til søs 1870-1911* (Copenhagen, 1987).

Table 1
Monthly AB Wages in Eight North Sea Ports, 1880-1900

Year	LON £/mo.	DUN Index	ANT Index	ROT Index	HAM Index	COP Index	GOT Index	TØN Index
1880	2.16	116	132	138	130	120	113	88
1881	2.44	95	118	125	111	116	97	71
1882	2.84	94	104	108	94	91	86	80
1883	2.73	99	108	113	104	98	95	88
1884	3.00	98	98	101	93	92	90	82
1885	2.16	115	137	145	141	127	126	100
1886	2.17	116	129	145	138	127	114	91
1887	2.08	125	131	148	154	126	116	98
1888	2.11	119	136	147	156	127	118	106
1889	3.06	95	109	106	106	91	87	87
1890	3.08	95	106	106	109	95	90	91
1891	3.08	96	103	107	107	102	95	88
1892	3.04	98	101	110	104	106	95	85
1893	2.97	99	92	106	104	110	93	75
1894	2.61	104	115	121	115	128	103	89
1895	2.14	115	128	137	139	160	123	104
1896	2.15	112	133	137	152	163	130	104
1897	2.23	112	136	134	153	160	133	102
1898	2.24	115	129	135	146	156	137	108
1899	3.10	90	90	100	114	118	101	87
1900	3.00	95	100	109	120	127	110	95

Notes: LON = London; DUN = Dunkerque; ANT = Antwerp; ROT = Rotterdam; HAM = Hamburg; COP = Copenhagen; GOT = Gothenburg; and TØN = Tønsberg. London wages equal 100 in each year.

Source: Lewis R. Fischer, "Around the Rim: Seamen's Wages in North Sea Ports, 1863-1900," in Lewis R. Fischer, *et al.* (eds.), *The North Sea: Twelve Essays on Social History of Maritime Labour* (Stavanger, 1992), 59 ff.

Table 2
Growth of the Merchant Marines in Eight North Sea Countries, 1880-1900 (000 Nrt)

Year	France			Belgium			Netherlands			United Kingdom		
	Sail	Steam	Total	Sail	Steam	Total	Sail	Steam	Total	Sail	Steam	Total
1880	278	246	524	10	65	75	264	64	328	3851	2724	6575
1885	508	492	1,000	5	80	85	194	108	302	3457	3973	7430
1890	444	500	944	4	72	76	127	128	255	2936	5043	7979
1895	387	501	888	1	86	87	102	188	290	N/A	N/A	N/A
1900	510	528	1,038	1	113	114	78	268	346	2247	6917	9164

Year	Germany			Norway			Sweden			Denmark		
	Sail	Steam	Total	Sail	Steam	Total	Sail	Steam	Total	Sail	Steam	Total
1880	-	-	-	1461	58	1,519	462	81	543	198	52	250
1885	788	345	1,133	1449	114	1,563	407	110	517	180	90	270
1890	682	593	1,275	1503	203	1,706	370	141	511	182	112	294
1895	593	796	1,389	1284	321	1,605	302	181	483	179	144	323
1900	584	1319	1,903	1003	505	1,508	289	325	614	147	247	394

Note: The steam totals for France in 1880 were calculated by subtracting sail from total as there is evidently a misprint in Mitchell for the 1880 figure.

Source: B.R. Mitchell (comp.), *International Historical Statistics. Europe 1750-1988* (3rd ed., Hong Kong, 1992), table F4, 689-709.

The figures for the merchant marines of the various countries include both sail and steam. As Fischer provides wages only for the former, we should perhaps consider investment in sail separately. For the entire period 1880-1900, it was characteristic of all eight that steam tonnage grew while sail fell (France, however, was an exception, since its sail fleet actually grew between 1880 and 1900). The question thus is whether wages for ABs serving in sail were highest in nations that experienced the least reduction in such tonnage? In the 1880s French sail tonnage increased in general, and the Danish sail tonnage declined relatively slowly, while the largest reduction occurred in the Belgian fleet. The tentative hypothesis is not proved, since actual wages in Hamburg, Rotterdam, Antwerp and Copenhagen were higher on average than in Dunkerque, the only port which experienced an overall increase in its sailing fleet. The relatively low wages for ABs in Dunkerque are thus not explicable solely by the experience of French sail tonnage.

But what about the relation between Danish tonnage and wages? In the 1890s the relative decline of German sailing tonnage was less than the Danish, while the drop elsewhere was sharper. For the years 1893-1900 the development of tonnage does not explain the high wages in Copenhagen, since the Danish sailing fleet was among those that declined the most in those years.

On balance, there is no firm connection between demand and wage levels for ABs in sailing vessels between 1880 and 1900. Yet a closer inspection of one country may shed further light. In the following pages we analyze specific developments in Denmark.

The Danish Merchant Marine, 1879-1900

A small vessel requires more crew per ton than a larger one (tables 3a-3b). The Danish merchant marine added 355 vessels and 142,000 net registered tons (nrt) in the period 1879-1900. This was due to a large investment in steam, which increased by 291 vessels (198,000 nrt). Except for those between 200 and 299 nrt, all steam tonnage classes grew during the period. The most important growth occurred in the 1890s, primarily among steamers over 500 nrt. Moreover, in the 1890s the number and tons of sail were reduced considerably in all classes from twenty to 499 nrt. On the other hand, the number and tonnage of sail below twenty nrt and over 500 nrt – especially the smallest craft – expanded significantly. Despite a total reduction of more than 56,000 nrt, the increase in smaller sailing vessels meant that their numbers increased by sixty-four from 1879 to 1900. But did this phenomenon cause a concomitant need for men, especially in the critical 1890's?

Development in Tonnage and Requirement of Manning, 1890-1900

For the period in question there are no Danish figures comparable to the Finnish man/ton ratios calculated by Yrjö Kaukiainen.[3] By applying his model to a sample of Danish vessels with known crew sizes we established that the Finnish manning ratio per 100 nrt for sail under 500 nrt was slightly higher than the Danish, while for sailing ships above 500 nrt it was slightly lower. As there were no steamers above 700 nrt in Kaukiainen's material, comparable calculations were done on Danish steamers in the 1890s using Kaukiainen's man/ton ratio for 1905. Since these also showed a close congruence, it is fairly safe to use the Finnish man/ton ratios to derive crew requirements for the fleet. It must be stressed, however, that the result will be slightly lower than the actual figure, since Kaukiainen did not include vessels under twenty nrt. For them, we made a spot check of 300 vessels in *Danmarks Handels-Flåde* for 1897. These craft have been sorted by type, the crew size found from known examples, and a calculation of man/ton ratios made (see table 4).

The table reflects the same pattern as table 3. In the sail fleet there was a generally lower crew requirement through the 1890s for all vessels except those over 1000 or under twenty nrt. Total crew in the sail fleet was reduced by 1820 in the years 1890-1900. On the other hand, steam manning increased for all vessels except those between 200 and 300 nrt. The most significant rise was for ships over 1000 nrt, which demanded an additional 1774 men. The total manning requirement for the steam fleet rose by 2927, which meant that the total manning for the Danish merchant fleet in the years 1890-1900 grew from 14,695 to 15,802.[4]

---

[3]Yrjö Kaukiainen, *Sailing into Twilight. Finnish Shipping in an Age of Transport Revolution, 1860-1914* (Helsinki, 1991), table 2.25.

[4]The calculations may be compared with the number of persons from the 1901 census working at sea (18,066 persons); *Statistisk Tabelværk*, 5. rk., lit. A, nr. 4 Folketællingerne i Kongeriget Danmark d. 1. Februar 1901, Anden del, 1904. The difference between this number and the total in table 4 reflects three factors: Danish crews were slightly smaller than those in Finland; the proportion of Danish seamen serving on foreign ships is unknown; and many fishermen operated small craft not included in official statistics and therefore not included in the calculations in table 4.

Table 3a
The Danish Merchant Marine, Sail, Relative to Size, 1879-1900

Year	4-19 nrt No.	4-19 nrt NRT	20-99 nrt No.	20-99 nrt NRT	100-199 nrt No.	100-199 nrt NRT	200-299 nrt No.	200-299 nrt NRT	300-499 nrt No.	300-499 nrt NRT	500-699 nrt No.	500-699 nrt NRT	700-999 nrt No.	700-999 nrt NRT	Over 1000 nrt No.	Over 1000 nrt NRT
1879	1265	12428	927	46226			680	108387	62	22281			19	13839	-	-
1889	1441	14269	912	40831			500	86643	65	24682			16	10601	4	4413
1890	1521	14872	947	41584	380	54041	116	28262	62	23399	19	11271	5	4423	4	4292
1891	1542	14991	964	42212	373	52697	117	28579	61	23606	27	15790	5	4361	5	5528
1892	1553	14992	971	42204	371	52482	111	27358	64	24295	30	17505	6	5044	8	9220
1893	1565	15121	973	42192	352	49673	114	28202	64	24384	32	18516	7	5809	9	10756
1894																
1895	1711	15846	785	34048	303	42421	100	24816	61	23270	33	19556	6	4830	11	14119
1896	1743	15873	770	33052	292	41033	93	23127	51	19259	32	18876	7	5611	12	15706
1897	1776	16264	772	32677	270	38023	87	21680	44	16459	28	16456	6	4630	13	16742
1898	1800	16352	784	33443	270	38026	85	21033	37	14173	25	14756	6	4630	13	16742
1899	1841	16696	779	31939	268	38047	81	20188	37	14115	23	13647	6	4911	12	15650
1900	1861	16883	761	31218	256	36758	69	17197	32	11897	20	11927	5	4308	13	16712

Notes: For 1879 and 1889, 200-299 nrt class includes 100-199 nrt vessels and 700-999 nrt class includes all vessels over 500 nrt for both sail and steam.
Source: See text.

Table 3b
The Danish Merchant Marine, Steam, Relative to Size, 1879-1900

Year	4-19 nrt No.	4-19 nrt NRT	20-99 nrt No.	20-99 nrt NRT	100-199 nrt No.	100-199 nrt NRT	200-229 nrt No.	200-229 nrt NRT	300-499 nrt No.	300-499 nrt NRT	500-699 nrt No.	500-699 nrt NRT	700-999 nrt No.	700-999 nrt NRT	Over 1000 nrt No.	Over 1000 nrt NRT
1879	45	507	45	2517			48	8495	16	6041						
1889	71	853	46	2399			78	14283	31	12213			38	31240	31	39240
1890	67	833	51	2532	46	6311	38	9389	34	13495	23	13256	48	34591	33	42010
1891	76	905	53	2565	49	6926	38	9359	38	15028	26	15138	30	24619	33	42010
1892	80	962	50	2434	50	7134	41	10194	38	15245	26	15295	30	24718	33	41829
1893	82	997	51	2451	51	7284	43	10713	39	15733	27	15956	31	25448	37	49010
1894													32	26579		
1895	101	1033	51	2663	58	8213	36	8879	44	17774	30	17586	41	34009	40	53902
1896	99	1025	56	2898	58	8181	35	8615	46	18701	32	19508	42	35455	50	68788
1897	102	1075	62	3117	58	8228	31	7490	47	19062	34	21253	42	35693	60	84791
1898	105	1054	68	3369	56	7969	31	7527	51	20545	38	23866	49	41854	78	116950
1899	106	1065	70	3546	59	8410	26	6356	48	19265	40	25236	58	49469	88	140653
1900	101	1079	70	3504	55	7820	27	6649	46	18341	41	25790	57	48770	86	135400

Notes: See table 3a.
Source: See table 3a.

Table 4
Calculated Manning Needs in the Danish Merchant Marine, 1890-1900

Year	Under 20	20-99	100-199	200-299	300-499	500-699	700-999	1000 +	Total Over 20	Total
Sail										
1890	2903	3243	2539	1045	655	296	75	64	7917	10820
1891	2926	3292	2476	1057	660	331	74	82	7972	10898
1892	2926	3291	2466	1012	680	367	85	138	8039	10965
1893	2952	3290	2334	1043	682	388	98	161	7996	10948
1894										
1895	3093	2655	1993	918	651	410	82	211	6920	10013
1896	3098	2578	1928	855	539	396	95	235	6626	9724
1897	3175	2548	1787	802	460	345	78	251	6271	9446
1898	3192	2530	1787	778	396	309	78	251	6129	9321
1899	3260	2491	1788	747	395	287	84	235	6027	9287
1900	3296	2435	1727	636	333	250	73	250	5704	9000
Steam										
1890	209	336	429	647	593	371	492	798	3666	3875
1891	228	341	470	645	661	423	494	798	3832	4060
1892	242	323	485	703	670	428	508	794	3911	4153
1893	251	325	495	739	692	446	531	931	4159	4410
1894										
1895	260	354	558	612	782	492	680	1024	4502	4762
1896	258	385	556	594	822	546	709	1306	4918	5176
1897	270	414	559	516	838	595	713	1611	5246	5516
1898	265	448	541	519	903	668	837	2222	6138	6403
1899	269	471	572	439	847	706	989	2672	6696	6965
1900	271	466	531	458	807	722	975	2572	6531	6802

Source: See text.

Table 5
Regional Distribution of Tonnage Relative to Ship Size and Means of Propulsion, 1879-1899

Sail		4-19 nrt		20-49 nrt		50-99 nrt		100-199 nrt		200-299 nrt		300-499 nrt		500-699 nrt		700-999 nrt		Over 1000 nrt	
		no.	ton.	no.	ton.	no.	ton.	no.	ton.	no.	ton.	no.	ton.	no.	ton.	no.	ton.	no.	ton.
Copenhagen	1879	100	963	48	1659	51	3763	82	16278			26	974	8	6005				
	1889	117	1148	59	3000	46	3095	49	9337	11	2789	4	1581	1	597			3	4061
	1899	186	1696	29	936	23	1760	24	3644			6	2087	2	1172				
Islands-east	1879	458	3857	164	5149	53	4032	135	22563			23	8142	10	7264				
	1889	538	4599	190	6433	30	2359	76	13404	12	2862	26	9245	4	2551	1	742	1	1091
	1899	644	5141	153	4851	30	2116	20	2561			4	1344	2	1112			1	1050
Islands-west	1879	333	3642	210	8909	200	15776	270	39258			7	2558						
	1889	298	3277	195	7929	157	12597	278	42838	35	8358	7	2600	1	569				
	1899	324	3097	217	7059	106	8334	210	29722			3	998						
Jutland	1879	374	3967	131	3827	70	5405	193	30288			6	2008	1	570				
	1889	487	5246	203	5854	32	2457	97	17065	23	6179	28	11256	11	7453	5	4169	3	3322
	1899	687	6762	206	5940	15	943	14	2120			24	9686	18	10794			8	10539

Steam		4-19 nrt		20-49 nrt		50-99 nrt		100-199 nrt		200-299 nrt		300-499 nrt		500-699 nrt		700-999 nrt		Over 1000 nrt	
Copenhagen	1879	23	237	6	219	15	1154	32	5310			10	3738	36	29954			30	38130
	1889	26	275	7	234	7	554	31	5384	8	1829	17	6893	44	31864	53	44958	85	137173
	1899	39	416	16	480	15	1213	19	2696			27	11030	30	19260				
Islands-east	1879	9	107	6	218	6	446	8	1506			3	1051	1	644				
	1889	20	258	7	239	8	555	16	3212	8	1993	7	2691	3	2104	1	968	1	1110
	1899	19	197	3	86	8	624	15	2114			9	3237	2	1147			1	1020
Islands-west	1879	4	46	5	145	2	149	2	510										
	1889	10	134	6	164	2	146	7	1179			1	413	1	685				
	1899	21	191	8	286			7	1037										
Jutland	1879	9	118	4	122	1	65	6	1170			3	1253	1	643				
	1889	15	187	5	172	4	337	24	4509	10	2534	7	2630	1	623	4	3543	2	2460
	1899	27	261	14	405	6	452	18	2563			12	4998	8	4829				

Source: See text.

Table 6
Manning Need Relative to Region and Means of Propulsion, 1879-1899

Year	Copenhagen			Islands-east			Islands-west			Jutland		
	Sail	Steam	Total	Sail	Steam	Total	Sail	Steam	Total	Sail	Steam	Total
1879	1768	1890	3658	2879	299	3178	4387	90	4477	2896	222	3118
1889	1059	2487	3546	2455	612	3067	4033	199	4232	2902	591	3493
1879	959	5168	6127	1863	638	2501	3552	157	3709	2913	1002	3915

Source: See text.

Still, this was hardly enough to require a pay increase for seamen who signed-on in Copenhagen. Thus, we now have two questions: did the development in tonnage and manning in Copenhagen differ from the rest of Denmark? If so, can different regional manning demands be the reason for various wage levels in Denmark? To answer these questions we must try to examine tonnage and manning patterns in various regions over the period.

Danish Regional Development of Tonnage and Manning, 1879-1899

In table 5 the development in the Danish merchant fleet has been grouped by size and propulsion into four regions: Copenhagen; the islands east of the Great Belt (Zealand, Lolland, Falster, Møn and Bornholm); the islands west of the Great Belt (Funen, Langeland and Ærø); and Jutland. Two regions (Copenhagen and Jutland) were growth areas; by contrast, the islands were in decline. In all regions steam tonnage grew, although expansion was greatest absolutely in Copenhagen and relatively in Jutland. The eastern and western islands grew less rapidly. The majority of steamers were registered in Copenhagen, where by 1899 they comprised 92.4% of the entire fleet. At the same time, 34.5% of the vessels owned in the eastern islands were steamers compared to 27.8% in Jutland and only 4.3% in the western islands. It is also worth noting that Jutland was the only region to have expanding investment in sail over the period as a whole, especially among vessels less than fifty and over 500 tons. In the other regions sail tonnage declined. This fall was sharpest in the eastern islands and Copenhagen and least pronounced in the western islands.

This varied development of the merchant fleet in the various regions was reflected in differential manning requirements (see table 6). The areas with growing demands for labour were, not surprisingly, Copenhagen and Jutland, while the two island groups had declining needs. Yet in all four regions there was an increase in the demand for labour to serve on steamers; as with tonnage, the absolute demand was strongest in Copenhagen while relative demand was more obvious in Jutland. In sail, the most powerful demand for labour was in Jutland, which was also the only region to have stable manning requirements. The need for crews in the eastern and western islands declined significantly, while in Copenhagen it was halved. The question is whether these differences influenced wage levels.

Danish Wages for Sailors, 1880-1900

Ideally an investigation of wages for Danish sailors should comprise all four regions. Unfortunately, the seamen's employment bureaus in the conscription or customs offices were quite erratic in handling crew lists, and often these documents have been destroyed. This is particularly true for Jutland, where only the districts of Ebeltoft, Hjørring and Sæby have preserved crew lists, and wage information is found in only a handful of instances. Indeed, only the lists of the conscription office of Aalborg contain useful material. Outside of Jutland, only for Nakskov, Helsingør (Elsinore), Odense and Svendborg is there sufficient information.[5] Table 7 presents the material for the provincial ports as well as Fischer's wage series for Copenhagen.

Table 7
Mean Wages for ABs Recruited in Copenhagen and Provincial Ports, Sail, 1880-1900 (DKK)

	1880	1885	1890	1895	1900	Mean Cases/Year
Svendborg	38.9	45.1	51.4	50.7	58.1	14
Helsingør	38.6	40.2	50.7	50.0	-	12
Nakskov	48.0	44.6	51.6	51.3	59.7	10
Odense	-	-	-	-	55.5	23
Aalborg	-	-	-	46.4	58.6	12
Copenhagen	46.8	49.5	52.6	61.6	68.6	118

Notes: Svendborg figures are based on a random sample while those for the other districts include all cases for particular years. The low number of ABs joining in ports like Aalborg is a function of the fact that most ships calling at that port were steamers.

Sources: Helsingør, Nakskov and Odense: Seamen's employment bureaus (*mønstringsruller*); Svendborg and Aalborg: Conscription offices (*udskrivningskredse*); Copenhagen: Fischer, "Around the Rim," 59-73.

---

[5]Landsarkivet for Nørrejylland, 5. Udskrivningskreds, Mønstringsprotokol (Sporteljournal) for Aalborg (1894-1903) B422-513; Landsarkivet for Fyn 3. Udskrivningskreds, Mønstringsprotokol (Sporteljournal) for Svendborg (1874-1903); Landsarkivet for Sjælland, Lolland-Falster og Bornholm, Helsingør Toldkammer M-12, M-13, M-14, M-16 (1874-1901), Nakskov Toldkammer M-1 (1870-1912).

Through the entire period the largest hiring places for seamen in the provinces – Aalborg, Helsingør and Svendborg – had lower wages than Copenhagen. The fourth port – Nakskov – in 1880 had slightly higher pay than Copenhagen, but later fell back to the level of the other provincial ports. There is no ready explanation of this difference. It may be that provincial shipowners took advantage of a modest local competition for labour or that family relations helped them squeeze the payroll (it is often told how the skippers of Marstal in the Baltic hired low-paid relatives). Although to test such hypotheses requires more than we can presently handle, a cursory examination of the data suggests that the family explanation does not apply to Aalborg and Helsingør, where most seamen were from other parts of the country or abroad.

Thus far, our research has established that there is no apparent relationship between the development of national merchant marines and the unit cost of labour. Moreover, we have established that there was a significant premium paid to maritime labour in Copenhagen compared to provincial ports. The labour costs of the capital were generally higher and require no specific explanation in the national context. But we may ask why masters were willing to pay a premium substantially above other major North Sea ports. This raises the issue of the total labour pool available in various ports, as well as the issue of shipping patterns and the changing logistics of international shipping in the period. It is conceivable that the free port status of Copenhagen, achieved in 1894, may have attracted more ships and thus raised wages.[6] But a full investigation of such issues is outside the scope of this essay.

Earnings in the Fishing Industry

The total Danish maritime labour force in 1901 was 18,066 persons, almost half of whom were fishermen.[7] In a previous article one of the

---

[6]Unfortunately, the shipping lists do not include ships that were not inspected by the customs as well as ships for orders. Consequently, there is no immediate way to substantiate the hypothesis. The customs lists show no increase in ship clearances in the port of Copenhagen during the 1890s (*Statistisk Tabelværk* 1890-1900; concerning the question of ships not included in the statistics, see footnote for the 1900 publication).

[7]See footnote 4 above. The number of fishermen must be an approximation. *Fiskeri-Beretning 1900-1901* lists the number of fishermen per district which may be summed up to 7460 full-time fishermen. The 5818 part-timers were listed in the census under

authors has documented the vigorous rise of fishing incomes when deck fishing was introduced.[8] Esbjerg fishermen, for example, earned yearly incomes twenty percent or more above average yearly wages of Norwegian seamen (the Norwegian series was chosen because comparable Danish material was unavailable). Unfortunately, the lack of wage information from the Esbjerg-Fanø district makes it impossible to test directly the relationship between high fishing incomes after 1880 and seamen's wages.[9] But thus far the international discussion of maritime labour markets has not considered the impact of fishing – or any competing maritime industry – on the demand for ABs. If in Denmark there were a high demand for such men in fishing – and if such men were paid considerably more than their colleagues in shipping – we might expect the maritime labour market to have reflected this pressure. It therefore seems logical to examine earnings in the fishing industry in some detail.

Fishing statistics are today often unreliable because fishermen frequently try to conceal their actual catches and financial status from authorities with a fiscal or biological interest in their activities. A century ago, statistics were collected to promote the national fishing effort and paradoxically are thus much more reliable. The more progressive fishermen often received state loans to invest in new ships and were obliged to render accounts to be printed in the official *Fiskeri-Beretning*.

---

their main occupation, some of them no doubt were sailors.

[8]Poul Holm, "Fishermen's Shares and Maritime Wages in Scandinavia, 1880-1910," *International Journal of Maritime History*, IV, No. 2 (1992), 219-226.

[9]A few ledgers for Fanø sailing vessels have survived: see Morten Hahn-Pedersen and Holger Munchaus Petersen, *Prinsen og Prinsessen – to storsejlere fra Fanø* (Esbjerg, 1989), 18, and Morten Hahn-Pedersen, "Bark *Killeena* af Sønderho. En brik i søfartshistoriens puslespil," *Sjæk'len 1993* (Esbjerg, 1994), 91-113. The evidence does not suggest that high incomes in the fisheries influenced wages in the shipping industry. The barque *Prinsesse Marie*, for example, paid its seven sailors DKK 48.7 per month on average when hiring a new crew in Helsingør in June 1893. The barque *Killeena* in 1894 paid only DKK 39 per month for the four sailors recruited in Hamburg. Indeed, the second mate was paid only DKK 62. The crew of the two ships was the usual blend of seamen from the home island, elsewhere in Denmark and abroad. Modest as this material is, it does not suggest that the much higher incomes in the local fishing industry greatly affected merchant shipping. Instead, the Fanø seamen got the same pay as those on Svendborg ships (or even fared worse). The two wage agreements were even lower than the average for the two ports in question.

This information is generally sound, but is of course biased towards the best sectors of the fisheries. In addition, the total catch and marketing of fish was recorded by local harbour authorities or an entrusted person. These records are of varying reliability, but generally the information seems to have been collected meticulously and enthusiastically. A consecutive series on the income of ABs in cutter fishing can be reconstructed from these records. The material was collected from 1881 for the use of the fisheries' councillor in the Ministry of Internal Affairs. It, too, was published from 1889 in the *Fiskeri-Beretning*. At a minimum the reports gave the total value of catches and numbers of vessels and men in specific fishing districts.

The west coast of Jutland was only covered in the *Fiskeri-Beretning* from 1892, but the local records office in Esbjerg has information collected by the customs officer, Lorck-Madsen, from 1881 onwards on the activities of the then largest fishing village on the west coast, Hjerting, ten kilometres north of Esbjerg. In 1870, one-third of the male work force in Hjerting served on deep-sea sailing vessels from the nearby island of Fanø. Hjerting lacked larger vessels and local capital was employed in Fanø vessels. By 1890, the census showed a growing population and almost every man (ninety people) was registered as a fisherman. The vessels were owned by one or two fishermen together with local merchants and innkeepers.[10] Traditionally, the fishermen had operated open boats with crews of seven who split the catch equally. But with the introduction of decked vessels in the 1870s, the capital accruing in long-lining was concentrated in the hands of the boatowners, as the share system was still reckoned on the basis of the old open-boat system of seven shares; four for the fishermen and three for the boatowners. The vast increase in productivity thus was almost wholly absorbed by the boatowning fishermen and people ashore. Nevertheless, fishermen could earn a much better income than their fellow seamen in the merchant marine (see table 8). It is therefore hardly surprising that the Hjerting seafarers withdrew from the Fanø fleet and built up their own fishing fleet in a brief period of time. The long-line fisheries off Hjerting signalled a breakthrough for decked vessels in Denmark; in the mid-1880s this open-coast launching site was one of the country's leaders.

---

[10]Poul Holm, *Hjerting – en maritim landsby midt i verden, 1550-1930* (Esbjerg, 1992).

Table 8
Earnings of Hjerting Fishermen, 1881-1899

Hjerting	No. of vessels	No. of men	Average Crew	Total Catch	Total share ABs per year	Monthly share on 8 months fishing, ABs
1881	12.0	38	3.2	24,600	366.1	45.8
1882	12.0	38	3.2	32,600	485.1	60.6
1883	17.0	54	3.2	63,100	662.8	82.9
1884	18.0	58	3.2	65,310	647.9	81.0
1885	20.0	59	3.2	75,855	677.3	84.7
1886	22.0	80	3.2	72,983	592.4	74.0
1887	23.0	81	3.2	78,761	611.5	76.4
1888	23.0	81	3.2	67,494	524.0	65.5
1889	21.0	67	3.2	65,523	557.2	69.6
1890	20.0	63	3.2	49,026	437.7	54.7
1891	19.0	60	3.2	55,230	526.0	65.8
1892	19.0	56	2.9	54,426	555.4	69.4
1893	19.0	57	3.0	68,638	688.1	86.0
1894	19.0	57	3.0	66,649	668.2	83.5
1895	16.0	56	3.5	42,959	438.4	54.8
1896	17.0	56	3.3	73,593	750.9	93.9
1897	18.0	58	3.2	50,955	502.0	62.8
1898	17.0	56	3.3	49,264	502.7	62.8
1899	19.0	68	3.6	43,195	363.0	45.4

Source: Byhistorisk Arkiv, Esbjerg (BA), Lorck-Madsen Fiskeristatistik (LMF).

The high earnings of fishermen were not just a phenomenon of Jutland. Increased income followed closely the success of new fishing equipment, such as the use of seine nets to catch plaice, developed for the sheltered waters of the Limfiord at mid-century and introduced to the Kattegat in the mid-1870s. Seines became so popular that they were used by merchant vessels in south Funen that shifted from shipping to fishing. Contemporary records verify that such experiments were very successful.[11] The attraction of seining was that it offered a young fisherman the

---

[11]In 1885 six vessels from Thorøhuse, and one each from Brunshuse and Assens, went seine fishing for plaice in the Kattegat for five months. The boats were from seven to 18.5 tons burthen and each had a crew of four. The yield was 40-50,000 scores of

possibility of earning enough in a few years to invest in his own boat. The calculation of shares on a seiner was done in a manner very attractive to the non-owner. The crew consisted of four or five fishermen, each allotted a share, with only one share reserved for the boat. The boat's share would be divided between the boatowners, normally the skipper and one fisherman and perhaps one participant ashore. This returned the share system to "normal," after the boatowners had feasted under the Hjerting regime.

A count in 1885 of the entire commercial fishing industry in the Kattegat showed that 699 men on seventy-six cutters and 124 smaller vessels caught fish valued at DKK 578,329.[12] On the basis of one share per vessel and one share per fisherman the earnings divide into 899 parts worth DKK 644 per part. If the fishing season were six months on average, the result was DKK 107/month per part (DKK 92 if the season lasted seven months). The average fisherman would thus earn nearly twice as much as the ordinary sailor. While a seaman could hope for a longer employment period to raise his yearly income, so too could the fisherman, although not of course with the same earnings per month as when fishing.[13]

A search of Danish repositories has revealed that only one balance sheet for a fishing vessel before 1900 seems to have been preserved. This comes from Harboøre in west Jutland, where one cutter

---

plaice worth DKK 28-30,000, which was divided equally among the four men plus one share for the vessel. In other words, one share amounted to DKK 750 for five months' work, or DKK 150 per month. This was unusually good, but other information confirms that fish were extremely plentiful in domestic waters in these years. In the long-run, however, these vessels were ill-suited for seining and the fishing grounds were too distant. We do not know what happened to these fishermen in the 1890s (*Dansk Fiskeriforenings Medlemsblad 1886*, 78).

[12]*Ibid.*, 82.

[13]The good conditions for the fishing industry were stable through the 1880s if a survey of smack fishing from Hornbæk in the Kattegat can be taken as representative. In 1881 there was just one smack with five men in that fishery earning DKK 124/month for the six months from March to August. The following year four smacks with twenty-one men took part – they had a rather poor result of DKK 68/month. In 1883 another vessel entered, and the result was remarkably better – DKK 94/month – for a season that lasted seven months. Similar earnings were generated by six smacks with thirty-one men the following year, while the same number in 1885 had an income of only DKK 77/month for seven months. In 1886 seven smacks made DKK 84/month (*Ibid.*, 167).

in 1894 paid shares of DKK 622 per crew member for seven months of fishing with a cutter in the Kattegat and North Sea; the result works out to DKK 89 per month. The accounts also reveal that the crew did some fishing at home during the winter worth DKK 355 per person. If the individual fisherman did not have other income during the remaining two winter months, his annual earnings worked out to a monthly income of DKK 81.41 a month, or one-third more than a fully-employed seaman. No wonder that the fisherman in charge of the accounts remarked dryly that he was "quite satisfied" with the results.[14]

The fishermen had revolutionized their trade in the Kattegat in the 1880s. In the mid-1890s the scene shifted to the North Sea; in the forefront were men from the north Jutland port of Frederikshavn. We know that the years around 1890 were relatively poor in the Kattegat fishing industry, and their meagre returns for that year (table 9) fit the picture. Although seine fishing for a couple of years regained the position it had enjoyed in the 1880s, the extremely poor returns of 1893 provided the economic backdrop for the shift to the North Sea. During the latter half of the 1890s the settlement of shares aboard Frederikshavn seiners was very good.

The Frederikshavn example soon inspired colleagues in Esbjerg, where local fishermen would often see them land good catches. The results of the Esbjerg fishermen, also summarized in table 9, show modest earnings up to mid-decade, when their results were still overshadowed by the long-line fishermen from neighbouring Hjerting (a fact noticed at the time). Only in 1894 did a fish monger set up a direct sale of fresh plaice from Esbjerg to Hamburg and induce local fishermen to begin seining in earnest. By 1897 the Esbjerg fishermen were earning as much as the Hjerting people who stuck to long-lining, and Esbjerg soon outdistanced its rival. Indeed, over the next few years the success of the Esbjerg seine fishery induced hundreds of fishermen to move permanently or semi-permanently to the town. In a decade, Esbjerg became Denmark's premier fishing port. The success of Esbjerg seining almost extinguished the Hjerting fishery. Hjerting landed two-thirds of all catches in 1890, but less than ten percent by 1900 and only two percent by 1910. Most fishermen moved to Esbjerg and took up seining.

---

[14]Published in Anders Vrist Langer, *Fiskerdagbøger fra Harboøre. 1. Tradition og fornyelse* (2 vols., Struer, 1988).

Table 9
Shares, Seiner Cutters from Frederikshavn and Esbjerg, 1890-1900

Year	Frederikshavn		Esbjerg	
	No. reports	Calculated share/month	Total no. boats	Calculated share/month
1890	13	74.8	18	50.7
1891	17	108.3	-	-
1892	15	102.6	-	-
1893	12	53.3	-	-
1894	14	98.7	-	-
1895	13	96.1	29	50.5
1896	9	114.7	32	73.8
1897	46	102.4	36	79.4
1898	29	118.5	43	73.7
1899	27	113.4	46	83
1900	26	75.9	50	82

Sources: Frederikshavn: *Fiskeri-Beretning*, 1890-1900; Esbjerg: BA, LMF.

The Flight from Shipping to Fishing in Hjerting, Esbjerg and Fanø

A good example of the shift from shipping to fishing was AB Lambert Sørensen of Hjerting. Born in 1842, he spent the first fifteen years of his adult life on the seven seas, but in 1870-1871 he participated in hook-and-line fishing on an American vessel off Newfoundland with a mostly Norwegian crew. He heard them talk of the supreme qualities of the Norwegian decked pilot boat and decided to introduce this craft when he retired to his home village. When he returned home in 1872, his success was instant, as he proved that three or four men in a decked vessel could catch the same amount per day as seven men in an open boat with safer journeys and more fishing days. In a few years Hjerting experienced a fishing boom and its sailors withdrew from the Fanø fleet to fish at home. The example was not lost on their Fanø comrades.

Fanø's historian, N.M. Kromann, was aware of the shift from shipping to fishing:

> The mid-1870s – and especially the end of the decade – were poor times for seafaring, and several seamen from Fanø turned to fishing and that old trade caught on,

yielded well and was run with great enthusiasm; they fished as in the past with trays and lines, built larger fishing vessels of types like the Norwegian pilot boats in which three or four men were needed. You invested much money, hoping it would turn out to be a profitable trade as a substitute to the poor earnings in shipping.[15]

Similarly, Lorck-Madsen commented in the local daily on Fanø's expanding fishing fleet:

It should be noted that these six boats have all been acquired by young able seamen [first mates] who have left the merchant marine to go fishing. More will doubtless follow their example. As they are not-so-well-off mates who because of low savings have no prospect of becoming captains, state subsidies would no doubt contribute to gather able and young forces for the fishing of Fanø, which has all the chances of creating a capable and energetic fishing population.[16]

After a recession at the beginning of the 1880s the fishery increased again until 1887, when there were fifty-four men on fourteen vessels ranging from four to twenty-nine tons burthen. They sold most of their catch to Hamburg. After 1890 the number of line fishermen was reduced rapidly, but from the mid-1890s it rose again. Now it was seine fishing that attracted the seamen of Fanø either to enlist on Esbjerg vessels or to join one of the thirteen seiners registered on Fanø after the turn of the century. In the *Fiskeri-Beretning* attention was devoted to the fact that fishing and shipping were in competition on Fanø. In 1890 it was noted that the decline in fishing that occurred that year most likely was to be "accredited to the better paying business, which could now be offered able-bodied seamen, who were natives of Nordby, especially after the latest increase in the merchant fleet of Fanø."[17]

---

[15]N.M. Kromann, *Fanøs Historie* (3 vols., Esbjerg, 1934), II, 106.

[16]*Vestjyllands Dagblad*, 6 February 1887.

[17]*Fiskeri-Beretning for Finantsaaret 1890-1891* (Copenhagen, 1892), 82.

The evidence shows that this was a short-lived revival; a few years later the Fanø merchant fleet started a dramatic decline. From 1895 to 1905 its tonnage was reduced from 44,194 to 17,947 nrt. During this period a number of people shifted from shipping to fishing. Among the owners of fishing cutters on Fanø in 1898 was Søren Abrahamsen, who had abandoned the construction of large sailing vessels for the overseas trade in 1896. He had already built on Fanø a number of fishing vessels, and it was the construction of this type of vessel that became the basis of his future business – in Esbjerg. Apart from Abrahamsen, an examination of the ships in the *Fiskeri-Beretning* and the Fanø and Esbjerg customs records in the years 1880-1925 reveals the recycling of old ship names and the appearance of many investors formerly in Fanø shipping.[18] A full documentation of the flight from shipping to fishing, including men as well as capital, is a *desideratum* for future research.

Seamen Go Fishing off Iceland

The immense growth of English steam trawling during the 1880s motivated a group of Copenhagen and Esbjerg shipowners to try experimental fishing off Iceland in cooperation with some sail-cutter owners from Frederikshavn.[19] The crews of the steam trawlers comprised experienced Danish and English trawler skippers and naval officers as well as fishermen from the west coast of Jutland. Icelandic fishing made great demands on both stamina and navigation skills. It prompted the establishment of navigation schools for fishing masters, just as in the merchant marine. Yet from the beginning it was necessary to guarantee a fixed minimum pay to attract Danish and English fishermen to the trawlers. Information from company accounts show that seamen

---

[18]Morten Hahn-Pedersen, "Rise – Decline – Fall. The Shipping Trade on Fanø – A Comparative Analysis of the Period of Reorganisation and Final Collapse, 1860-1920," in Poul Holm and John Edwards (eds.), *North Sea Ports and Harbours – Adaptations to Change* (Esbjerg, 1992), 73-119.

[19]See Poul Holm, "Technology Transfer and Social Setting. The Experience of Danish Steam Trawlers in the North Sea and off Iceland, 1879-1903," in Holm (ed.), *Northern Seas Yearbook 1994* (Esbjerg, 1994), 113-157.

were paid DKK 100 per month in 1894.[20] This minimum wage strained company finances.

The sailing cutters from Frederikshavn, on the other hand, used the part share system. Contrary to the steam trawlers they made a profit, so they could attract domestic fishermen with the prospect of favourable incomes. Because of government subsidies, the shipping companies were obliged to publish details of their earnings in the *Fiskeri-Beretning*. The calculation of shares was done by percentages in this fishery. The percentage system is well documented in the fishery off Iceland and several cutter accounts have been preserved. These show that differences in wages occurred that were unknown under the share system. A seaman was paid approximately eight percent of the total catch after the deduction of certain expenses, such as ice and barrels.

Published accounts show that the *Prins Valdemar*, for example, earned a profit on its Icelandic fishing of DKK 9851. Of this, the ship took 24/52, the captain 8/52, the mate 6/52, the bosun 4/52 and three able seamen 3/52 each; 1/52 was divided equally among the crew. In cash terms, this meant that the captain earned DKK 1567, or DKK 258 per month, the mate DKK 194, the bosun DKK 132, and the three able seamen DKK 100 per month each. For the rest of the year the ship fished oysters in the North Sea, where it made half its profits. If the crew and income distribution were the same as above, the captain would have received an extra DKK 453, the mate DKK 340, the bosun DKK 226, and each AB DKK 170. In this way, an AB could earn DKK 1015 per year, or DKK 85 per month, which would have brought him to the same level as his colleagues fishing on cutters in the North Sea or the Kattegat. The Icelandic accounts for the other cutters show that the *Prinsesse Marie* did best, with a monthly share to ABs of DKK 144. The *Nordvest* paid DKK 102, while the *Emilie Franziska* only brought in DKK 98 per month.[21]

These examples demonstrate that rising wages in the domestic fishery forced wages up on deep-sea fishing vessels, including the steam trawlers that in reality could not justify such high wages. Steamship owners complained repeatedly about the high wages, which finally served as the excuse to give up fishing off Iceland. Explaining the failure of the

---

[20]*Fiskeri-Beretning 1895-1896*, 155.

[21]*Ibid.*, 155-160.

steam trawling company in 1902, one of the main instigators, C.F. Drechsel, insisted that the main problem had been the Danish fishermen:

> The greatest obstacle, however, is to be found in the fact that the Danish fishing community is not sufficiently interested in taking part in large-scale deep-sea fishing. Conditions in domestic waters are too good for the Danish fishermen, who are able with much less effort, and generally with much greater ease, to earn a good income fishing in more sheltered waters.[22]

With this remark Drechsel suggested that wages had been too high to allow for a profit, and that this had been because fishing in home waters paid so well.

An Integrated Maritime Labour Market in Denmark?

The result of this research is not as unambiguous as the authors could have hoped. The preliminary discussion of Fischer's material showed no real connections between wages and the development of the merchant fleets around the North Sea countries, either in terms of total carrying capacity or sailing ship tonnage.

An analysis of the extant evidence from five provincial ports – Aalborg, Svendborg, Odense, Helsingør and Nakskov – showed that wages were significantly lower in the provinces than in Copenhagen. The difference, which needs further research, appears to reflect the conjunction of aggregate supply and demand in individual ports. It goes without saying that Copenhagen – one of the largest ports-of-call in the Baltic trades – demanded large numbers of sailors both for steam and sail. Its designation as a free port in 1894 possibly induced so many ships to call that this in itself satisfactorily explains the sharp increase in wages from that year.

By dividing the Danish merchant fleet into four regions we observed a significant difference between Copenhagen – with a clear head start in steam – and the provincial ports that in general clung to sail. Nonetheless, Jutland differed from the ports on the islands, partly because of significantly better growth and in part due to continued

---

[22]*Fiskeri-Beretning 1901-1902*, 278-279.

investment in small sailing craft. While little wage information from Jutland has been preserved, the indications are that wages there paralleled the experience of the provinces rather than Copenhagen.

The small sailing vessels required relatively great inputs of labour and were primarily used for fishing. An analysis of the earnings in this industry shows that fishermen – not only in Jutland but also in the provinces – experienced a strong increase in earnings, especially with the introduction of decked boats and the seine net. Income was 50-100% above the mean for ABs in Danish ports. Many seamen and even some officers quit shipping for fishing. Well-documented examples of this exist in Fanø/Esbjerg, Frederikshavn and even the small islands off south Funen. Further research should include a quantitative study of this phenomenon.

Nevertheless, there was little wage pressure. Neither the significantly better earnings of the fishermen nor the relatively high wages in Copenhagen forced up wages in provincial ports. On the other hand, there was pressure on salaries in the deep-sea fishing industry as ABs and officers from the merchant marine and good fishermen – many with experience in English trawlers – were in great demand. During the years 1880 to 1900 the fishing fleet experienced unique wage increases in domestic waters. The high incomes in the inshore seine fisheries affected wages on steam trawlers in the Iceland fisheries, and shipowners blamed the high wages for the abandonment of this fishery.

The explanation for the lack of wage pressure in the shipping industry may rest in two possible areas. Perhaps there were sufficiently large sectoral barriers to prevent across-the-board wage increases – in other words, in spite of greater opportunities for better incomes in fishing, most seamen were deterred from becoming fishermen. The question, though, is whether such prejudices constitute a general explanation and if we can actually verify the magnitude of the shift from shipping to fishing? Regardless, another possibility is that there was such a surplus of maritime labour that despite the earnings in the fishing industry it was possible to hire seamen at lower pay for the merchant service. This explanation would lend weight to supply side arguments in discussions of the labour market and points to the need for research which, at least in Denmark, has been totally neglected.

The mechanisms used to keep wages low in the provinces should also be the subject of future studies. One factor to consider is the regulated career steps for navigational officers who by law had to be ABs before entering navigational schools. This requirement may have helped to keep wages low, since a prospective officer might temporarily tolerate poor wages. Later examples of this mechanism exist in Denmark and elsewhere.

In the period 1880 to 1900 the best paying career for an AB – who had little chance of becoming a captain in the merchant marine – would have been to get a navigation certificate in the merchant marine and then work his way up to bestman or master in the fishing industry. There might have been mental barriers in shifting from the merchant service to the fishery. Yet the attraction of high earnings and of being closer to the family probably overcame the scruples of many men and created the foundation for the remarkable growth of Danish fishing towns. From the late 1890s, navigation schools in the fishing towns prepared fishermen directly for careers in the fishery, and the twentieth-century labour market may have become less flexible.